Iron and Water

12/31/18

With best wishes to our good friends George & Joan.. I hope you enjoy my memoir !

IRON
and WATER

My Life Protecting
Minnesota's Environment

GRANT J. MERRITT

Grant Merritt

University of Minnesota Press
Minneapolis
London

Copyright 2018 by Grant J. Merritt

Published by the University of Minnesota Press
111 Third Avenue South, Suite 290
Minneapolis, MN 55401-2520
http://www.upress.umn.edu

ISBN 978-0-8166-7881-5

A Cataloging-in-Publication record for this book is available from the Library of Congress.

Printed in the United States of America on acid-free paper

The University of Minnesota is an equal-opportunity educator and employer.

24 23 22 21 20 19 18   10 9 8 7 6 5 4 3 2 1

For my parents, Glen and Alice Merritt

CONTENTS

PROLOGUE

I come from the worlds of iron and water. As a high school student in Duluth, Minnesota, my thoughts would drift during physics class, and I would absently gaze at iron ore boats stuck in the Lake Superior ice outside the ship canal. From my vantage point on the hill above the city, I could look down on Minnesota Point where, on winter days, huge shards of ice often piled up along the shore of the sand spit. This long stretch of sand offers a natural entrance to the Duluth–Superior harbor in Wisconsin. It is where my Merritt ancestors arrived at the headwaters of the lake in 1855 and 1856.

Some of the boats I observed carried new cars, presumably made from Mesabi Range iron ore. I often thought of my family heritage on the "Range" (as it is affectionately known) and the work and lives of my ancestors as trailblazers in the mining industry. I could also picture Isle Royale in my mind—the largest island in the world's largest lake where my family has had cabins for more than one hundred years. In my childhood, I fished and played there. I still do.

As a young boy, I learned to love the cold blue waters of Superior, its fogs, storms, and sparkling beauty on long summer days, and I naturally grew to hold an unwavering appreciation of the land and the water. My family history, coupled with a public school education that stressed student participation, provided the roots of my commitment to citizen advocacy in my adult life. I believe concerted, well-directed advocacy efforts are essential to restoring and preserving clean water and the environment. I also believe accurate historical documentation of environmental issues is critical to charting our course as stewards of natural resources.

On February 1, 1971, Governor Wendell Anderson appointed me executive director of the Minnesota Pollution Control Agency. Later that day, I received a phone call from a news reporter asking me to comment on my appointment. I remember saying at the time we were going to be pioneers in our work to clean up the environment.

In many ways, my work with the MPCA was very much connected with my ancestral history—the Merritt family who discovered and opened the first iron ore mine on the Mesabi Iron Range. I heard their stories from my father, and as a teenager read of their adventures in an account written by Paul de Kruif. Titled *Seven Iron Men*, it resonated with me then and has ever since. These oral and written accounts directly influenced my life choices. They taught me how a few citizens can make a big difference in the world, and their tenacious nature and legacy fueled my lifelong environmental passion as a lawyer and activist.

When I assumed my position with the state of Minnesota in 1971, Reserve Mining Company in Silver Bay, Minnesota, on the shore of Lake Superior was the largest taconite operation on earth, producing between ten and twelve million tons of iron pellets a year at an annual net profit in the millions.[1] The legislation that authorized the creation of the MPCA included a citizen policy-making board governing its decisions. This gave interested parties direct involvement in decisions on issues coming before the state agency. As a result, the controversial matters drew media attention that influenced public opinion on the Reserve case and many others. Aroused public sentiment led to the epic battle to stop Reserve Mining from fouling Lake Superior with sixty-seven thousand tons of taconite tailings per day. My role in the thirteen-year fight for a solution to the uncontrolled daily dumping of taconite tailings into Lake Superior would lead me directly into politics. Three years later I was working for the state of Minnesota.

Over the next ten years, I was directly involved in numerous political battles that have shaped Minnesota's modern history. I experienced some disappointments but also many victories. And where there were victories, my work was directly supported and affected by devoted citizen activists and public servants who helped achieve major policy decisions.

Reserve Mining was hardly the only menace Lake Superior and other freshwaters have faced during the past half century. Invasive species now pose a monumental threat to our waters. The damaging effect of climate change on the environment is readily apparent. Over the years, I have worked on environmental issues that included battles to prevent dumping of dredge spoils in Lake Superior and the Mississippi River, a three-year effort to stop the expansion of a large landfill adjacent to the Minnesota River, and a lawsuit attempting to enforce existing federal regulations preventing invasive species from entering Lake Superior in the ballast water of salt- and freshwater boats carrying cargoes to and from the various ports on the lake.

In order to meet the serious threats from pollution of the water, air, and land in Minnesota, I have often thought of the risks my grandfather and his brothers and nephews had taken in discovering iron ore on the Mesabi Range. The experience of my ancestors on the Mesabi also taught me the need to innovate just as they did in deciding how to mine a new type of iron ore, near the surface, which needed no shafts and could be scooped up with steam shovels. The history of my Merritt ancestors became for me a template of perseverance for pursuing on-land disposal of the Reserve taconite tailings.

The work of conservation is as crucial today as it was when I was a young environmental policy advocate. I've devoted a great deal of my lifework to assuring that clean water will be available to future generations. Obstacles were formidable then and remain so. The story of Reserve Mining is one of a pivotal battle and ultimate decision that altered environmental legislation on a national scale. It stands as a historic example and illustration of the power of citizen and political advocacy.

THE MERRITT FAMILY
AND THE MESABI
IRON RANGE

The Mesabi Iron Range

The Merritts first arrived at the head of Lake Superior from Chautauqua County, New York, in 1855 and 1856. My great-grandfather Lewis Howell Merritt and his oldest son, Napoleon, came in 1855 at the request of Edmund F. Ely, early missionary to the Indians, to supervise the construction of a sawmill in what is now Duluth at Fortieth Avenue West. Great-grandmother Hephzibah and her five sons arrived in 1856 and lived on a quarter section in Oneota, where the Merritts built the first hotel and schoolhouse. The mother of the Merritt boys was a small but sturdy woman born in 1812 who, according to my grandfather Alfred, was "universally beloved and ever helpful to the community."

There were eight Merritt boys in the family, five of whom grew up at the head of the lake. They attended the first school in the Duluth area, built by the boys' father, and were taught by their older brother, Jerome, the first schoolteacher in Duluth. While growing up, at least some of the boys became friends with the local Ojibwe Indians, especially Leonidas, who became a blood brother of Loon Foot.[1]

They worked different jobs around the waterfront, both in the woods and at the sawmill built by the Wheelers and the Merritts.

Alfred became interested in sailing and at nineteen worked as a deckhand on the schooner *Pierpont,* on which he visited Washington Harbor, Isle Royale, in 1866 to drop off fifteen hundred empty kegs for the fishermen there. They returned six weeks later and picked up the hundred-pound kegs, all full of salted lake trout, whitefish, and herring.

The next year, 1867, Alfred and his older brother Leonidas worked as chain men on the survey for the first railroad to reach Duluth, the Lake Superior and Mississippi. They built the first commercial vessel in Duluth, a forty-nine-ton schooner named the *Chaska,* which was sixty-seven feet long, and then built the schooner *Handy* to haul stone to the pier at the Superior Entry and the breakwater at Ontonagon, Michigan. They traded up and down both the north and south shores of Lake Superior, peddling flour, sugar, and salt among other food items.

Around this same time, in the winter of 1865–66, Lewis Howell Merritt joined the gold rush to Lake Vermilion, not far north from the Mesabi Range. On his way, some eighty teams of horses passed him, heading back to town along the Vermilion trail. After looking over the Vermilion property, he was not "boomed over the gold find." He was impressed, however, by the prospect of iron ore mining after being shown a chunk of iron ore by the blacksmith North Albert Posey. When he came home he told his sons that "someday there would be great mines discovered up in that region worth more than all the gold of California." Alfred would later say that "those words perhaps influenced us in later years to discover the Mesabi Range."[2]

Brothers Leonidas, Alfred, and Cassius worked in the woods around Duluth cutting white pine and prospered as lumberjacks. As they tramped through the muskeg swamps and among the white pine they remembered their father's words and looked for signs of iron ore. In the mid-1880s Cassius became head surveyor for the Duluth and Winnipeg Railroad. During the summer of 1887 he uncovered a large chunk of iron ore near the height of land, west of present-day Mountain Iron. The sample was taken to Duluth and

THE ORIGINAL PICTURE TAKEN 1871

TOP ROW: LEONIDAS MERRITT, FEBRUARY 20, 1844. LEWIS J. MERRITT, NOVEMBER 9, 1846. ANDRUS R. MERRITT, JUNE 22, 1853. ALFRED MERRITT, MAY 16, 1847. LUCIEN F. MERRITT, JUNE 12, 1859-SEPT, 28, 1900

BOTTOM ROW: CASSIUS CLAY MERRITT, JAN. 5, 1851-APRIL 27, 1894. HEPHZIBAH JEWETT MERRITT, OCT. 14, 1812-APRIL 16, 1906. LEWIS H MERRITT, JULY 9, 1809-MAR. 9, 1880 JEROME MERRITT, OCT. 3, 1832-OCT. 9, 1878 NAPOLEON B. MERRITT, APR. 19, 1834-MAR. 19, 1824

Lewis and Hephzibah Merritt and their eight sons. Alfred is my grandfather. Courtesy of the Minnesota Historical Society.

proved to be the first pure iron ore taken off the Mesabi Range. As a result Uncle Lon, Grandfather, and Cassius, joined by nephews Wilbur and John E., began an intensive, organized search for iron ore along Giant's Ridge, as the Mesabi Range is sometimes called. They hired men to dig test pits using shovels and, at times, the new diamond drills invented by Edmund J. Longyear. In March 1889 Alfred took a crew of six men to Mountain Iron. They traveled to Tower on the Duluth and Iron Range Railroad and left from there. They had "three dog trains and we were the dogs," Grandfather said in his autobiography. They focused on the south side of the Continental Divide, along the height of land on Giant's Ridge.[3]

On November 16, 1890, they found the first large body of rich hematite iron ore at what they called "Mountain Iron." Their crew chief, Captain James Nichols, immediately took a large sample of

3

the reddish, powdery ore to Duluth to have it assayed and it came out as 65 percent iron ore. The Mountain Iron Mine is now designated with a plaque as a U.S. historical landmark.

Shortly after the Merritt discovery, the assistant to the Minnesota State Geologist Horace V. Winchell said in his 1891 "report on the Mesabi Iron Range":

> The Merritt brothers, of Duluth and Oneota, were not to be discouraged by the reports of explorers and miners added to those of experts and geologists who had condemned the range ever since 1875. To these Duluth pioneers the Mesabi was an attractive and promising district and their faith in it was never shaken. . . . To them belongs the credit for persisting in the hunt for ore and the final discovery of it.[4]

The exciting days to follow were full of plans by the Merritts for further explorations on the Mesabi, and they acquired the Biwabik Mine, the Missabe Mountain Mine at Virginia, and others. At the same time they tried to convince the existing railroads—the Duluth and Iron Range, which went to the Vermilion Range from Two Harbors, the St. Paul and Duluth, and the Northern Pacific—to build tracks over to the Mesabi Range, but were unsuccessful. As a result, on February 11, 1891, the Merritts and four associates incorporated the Duluth, Missabe and Northern Railway Company (DM&N). A survey was completed and a construction contract signed for 48.5 miles of track from the Mountain Iron Mine to Stony Brook Junction, now known as Brookston.

The new railroad was completed by October 1892.[5] During this construction period, the Merritts turned to the Duluth and Winnipeg (D&W) and entered into a contract providing that the DM&N would build to Stony Brook Junction (about twenty-six miles west of Duluth), where it would then interline the iron ore with the D&W, proceeding over their tracks to the Allouez dock in Superior. The contract provided that the D&W would build 750 railroad cars and complete remaining work on its Allouez dock.[6]

While the DM&N was under construction, Henry W. Oliver of

Pittsburgh was in Minneapolis as a delegate to the 1892 Republican National Convention. There he heard talk of the activity taking place on the Mesabi Range and promptly took the train to Duluth and then on to Two Harbors, where he rode the Duluth and Iron Range Railroad north to Tower. From there he took the primitive road into Mountain Iron, where the Merritts showed him the Mesabi ore. Oliver quickly realized the potential of this rich iron ore and the result was the Merritts' first order for iron ore. Oliver was a steel man and contracted to purchase two hundred thousand tons of the "best quality blue ore, not to run lower than 63 percent iron or not over .05 percent phosphorous with delivery in 1893."[7] The DM&N was completed on time.

On October 15, 1892, the Merritts organized a special excursion for three hundred people, including fifty-five Merritts from Duluth, to the Mountain Iron Mine to celebrate the road's completion, and more importantly, their mother Hephzibah's eightieth birthday. Two days later the first train of iron ore from the Mesabi Range, powered by a steam locomotive pulling ten cars each filled with 20 tons, moved to the Allouez dock in Superior. This first cargo of Mesabi iron ore was loaded on November 1, 1892, into American Steel Barge No. 102, a whaleback ship designed by Alexander McDougall of Duluth. The whaleback then carried the 4,245 gross tons to Cleveland, Ohio.[8]

The Merritts Build into Duluth

Unfortunately for the Merritts, in the late fall of 1892 they learned the D&W was having financial distress and failed to live up to the contract to build 750 ore cars and complete the Allouez dock in Superior.[9] This breach of contract by the D&W was a leading factor in causing the Merritts to make what proved to be a fatal decision. They decided to build the railroad to Duluth themselves. This would prove significant because it required them to raise a considerable amount of capital in order to build the twenty-six-mile extension to Duluth and erect the first ore dock there.

This decision harmed the Merritts personally because it resulted in the link between them and the tycoon John D. Rockefeller. But the decision would be a good one for Duluth because it meant the creation of thousands of jobs in order to build the railroad to Duluth and the ore dock.[10]

After a favorable vote by the residents of St. Louis County in the spring of 1893, the Merritts borrowed $250,000 from the county, conditioned on building the DM&N into Duluth as well as an ore dock in the Duluth harbor. But more funds were needed to accomplish these two necessities. They attempted first to interest James J. Hill, owner of the Great Northern Railway (known as the Empire Builder), in helping them. He nearly did, but ultimately turned them down.

Historians advance two different reasons for Hill's rejection. According to David A. Walker, author of *Iron Frontier,* Hill was ready to aid the Merritts but only if he was sure Congress did not repeal the tariff on imported iron ore. A different version of Hill's refusal is contained in a Ph.D. dissertation by Joseph Wilmer Thompson titled "An Economic History of the Mesabi Division of the Great Northern Railway Company to 1915." According to Thompson, the Merritts had several meetings with Hill through an agent named Phillips, and Hill "wanted to aid the Merritts" but they required more money than Hill "could conveniently command."[11]

The Merritts then turned to Captain Alexander McDougall, a Duluth friend and inventor of the whaleback boat, who introduced them to C. W. Wetmore, vice president of the American Steel Barge Company. John D. Rockefeller had a substantial stock interest in the company. Wetmore had agreed to pay $450,000 to the Merritts within sixty days after signing the contract on December 24, 1892, but only $100,000 was paid. This was the beginning of the squeeze by the Rockefeller interests.

In the meantime, the DM&N, under President Alfred Merritt, worked furiously with a thousand men to lay the twenty-six miles of tracks into Duluth in four months, from March to July 1893. The ore dock reached 2,304 feet from the shore and contained eight thousand wooden pilings as well as 384 pockets each holding 175 tons of iron ore. This became the largest iron ore dock in the world at the time, and was built in only six months, from January to July 1893.

During this construction, the second worst depression in the country's history hit the United States. The stock market crashed on May 3, 1893, resulting in considerable additional strain on the Merritts. Wetmore continued to default as his installments came due. Leonidas Merritt spent months in New York meeting with Rockefeller's emissary Frederick T. Gates, the Baptist minister who had become a top aide to Rockefeller. Finally, Rockefeller proposed a consolidation of mining properties held by Rockefeller and the Merritts. The Rockefeller mines were the Spanish-American Iron Company in Cuba and two mines in Upper Michigan—the Penokee-Gogebic and the Aurora. Rockefeller claimed these properties were "gilt edged" and "large shippers of ore." The Merritts' contributions were nine mining properties, including the Mountain Iron, Missabe Mountain, and the Biwabik plus the DM&N railroad and the ore dock that had just been completed.

Before this consolidation became final in August 1893, most of the Merritt family assembled on the completed ore dock to witness the first trainload of Mesabi Range iron ore arriving in Duluth. On July 22, 1893, the train appeared on the tracks "like a black caterpillar creeping slowly along" the hillside toward the huge new ore dock out into the bay. "Nobody made a sound—not a hurrah or anything," wrote Leonidas's wife to her husband in New York City.[12]

There were many meetings in New York City, but only a short one between Leonidas and Rockefeller. The final deal provided Rockefeller with first mortgage bonds of the Lake Superior Consolidated Company, with the Merritts receiving stock. Unfortunately for the Merritts, this consolidated venture with Rockefeller did not solve their financial difficulties, nor did it stop the squeeze by Rockefeller and his associates from the American Steel Barge Company.

In January 1894 the Merritts were foreclosed by the Rockefeller interests with an "immediate payment" called upon five demand notes, totaling $432,575. Alfred went to see his friend in Duluth, Joseph Sellwood, and attempted to borrow this amount from the

Minnesota Iron Company of the Vermilion Range. When the answer came back by telegram, Sellwood told Grandfather, "My God, Alf, they won't do it!" Alfred soon learned the reason—Rockefeller had a controlling interest in that company as well.

When the Merritts could not make this payment, their collateral—which consisted of all their ore mines, the railroad, and the ore dock—all went to Rockefeller. On virtually the same date, the Penokee-Gogebic went bankrupt.[13]

After the foreclosure, Alfred Merritt sued Rockefeller on behalf of the family for fraud on the basis that Rockefeller had put his three ore properties into the Lake Superior Consolidated Iron Mines Company at fictitious values, which he knew were not "gilt edged" at the time the August 1893 agreement was signed.

In April 1893, four months before Rockefeller placed his three mines in this joint company with the Merritts, Gates sent a letter to J. D. Rockefeller's brother Frank Rockefeller stating that these three properties "were worthless." This letter was never produced in this litigation despite forty-nine exhibits, including some twenty-seven letters and telegrams that were produced by Rockefeller. If the Gates letter had been produced before or during the trial it would have been an "admission against interest" and there likely would have been an immediate settlement. Instead, it was buried in Rockefeller records and only showed up in the Rockefeller biography *Titan*, by Ron Chernow. It had been residing in the Allan Nevins collection at Columbia University. Chernow reports that there were two such letters, both concluding that Rockefeller's contributions to the Consolidated Company were "worthless."[14] Nevins knew about these letters because the researchers he employed made notes for Nevins based on these letters. Nevins never discusses the letters in his two-volume book on Rockefeller, *Study in Power*, which includes a full chapter on the Mesabi that is very favorable to Rockefeller.[15] Indeed, Nevins never bothered to come to Minnesota to get the Merritts' side of this involvement with Rockefeller, claiming he "didn't have the time," and he relied entirely on the Rockefeller archives and his side of the story.[16]

Alfred's lawsuit on behalf of the family sought $1,226,400. The trial before a jury in federal court in Duluth lasted eight days in June 1895. Rockefeller refused to appear, but Gates testified. On June 13, 1895, the jury awarded Alfred Merritt $940,000 in damages on the basis of Rockefeller's fraud.

Rockefeller appealed to the Eighth Circuit Court of Appeals in St. Louis, which in November 1896 reversed and remanded the case for a new trial, claiming there were errors in some of the instructions by Federal District Judge Riner and that the verdict amount exceeded the value of the Merritt properties. Having run out of money, the Merritts were forced to settle out of court for $525,000.

To get this settlement money, which they desperately needed to pay creditors, Rockefeller forced the Merritts to sign a full retraction, stating that Rockefeller had committed no fraud. They refused to sign for several months, but they finally capitulated. The settlement included an express agreement that the retraction would never be made public. Rockefeller had it published the very next day in papers all across the country, however. As one would expect, losing all their properties was a terrible blow to the Merritts. As Alfred later put it, "Naturally one will ask how did he do it. It was simply a case of our having confidence in [Rockefeller]. We were working away for the interests of the company, getting traffic contracts, fully trusting him. We woke up too late."[17] Being forced to sign the retraction was a final blow to the Merritts. It was presented by their former lawyer, Joseph Cotton, who had switched sides midstream and sold out to Rockefeller in becoming his counsel. My father wrote that Cotton "had the consummate gall and nerve to take this retraction to Father" before Rockefeller would pay the settlement amount agreed to months before.[18]

Sixteen years later, in 1911, a U.S. House of Representatives committee investigated the Steel Trust and held hearings in Washington, D.C., at the Capitol. It was formally designated as an investigation of U.S. Steel Corporation, but the committee also looked into the Rockefeller–Merritt transaction and allegations of fraud by the Merritts. Leonidas and Alfred testified at the hearings chaired by

Representative A. O. Stanley of Kentucky. Their testimony captured the interest of newspapers all around the country. Neither Rockefeller nor Gates testified before the committee, choosing instead to file a statement of rebuttal by Gates and later a pamphlet he published titled *The Truth about Mr. Rockefeller and the Merritts*. Neither the statement nor the pamphlet included the letter by Gates to Frank Rockefeller admitting that the mines Rockefeller put in the Consolidated Iron Mines Company were worthless. This is the letter Rockefeller's lawyers did not produce at the trial despite a formal request for production of all documents relating to the consolidation.

The fact that Rockefeller was not willing to testify and submit to cross-examination, as did Leonidas and Alfred, led Stanley to issue a statement strongly criticizing Rockefeller, which was carried by a large number of newspapers around the country. After the investigation, Stanley said "the people of Minnesota regarded these men [the Merritts], in a way, as we regard Boone in Kentucky, and as they regard Houston in Texas, with gratitude, with reverence."

Many years later, A. O. Stanley, who served Kentucky as U.S. representative, governor, and U.S. senator, came to Duluth for a hearing of the International Joint Commission on lake levels of Lake Superior. At that time in 1951, he was one of the three U.S. members of the IJC and its chairman. During his time in Duluth, he visited my father, in Duluth, where the picture of the two of them was taken. Stanley was interviewed by the *Duluth News Tribune* and had this to say about the history of the Mesabi Iron Range:

> The greatest contribution to national security and industrial development of America was made by three Duluth pioneers, Lon, Cass (Cassius) and Alf Merritt. . . . We have won two great wars, only because our fighting men were furnished lots of guns and ammunition made from Mesaba iron ore.[19]

On the hundredth anniversary of the discovery of the Mesabi Iron Range, on November 16, 1990, at Mountain Iron, Glen and Alice Merritt, my father and mother, and other Merritt family members assembled at the overlook of Mountain Iron. My father said:

If the Merritts had kept their holding it would have been a great thing for the State of Minnesota because that money would have stayed here; instead it was sucked into Pittsburgh and New York where Rockefeller lived. So Minnesota suffered a great loss when the Merritts lost their holdings on the Range because they would have been very, very rich men and could have done a lot for the State.[20]

My father used to say that "John D. Rockefeller was not only a crook but a fool." During the few months that the Lake Superior Consolidated Mining Company was under the control of the Merritts and Rockefeller, the Merritts tried to convince Frederick T. Gates that the company should buy the Wright and Davis lands that had been offered to the Merritts for $4.2 million. Gates only wanted to pay $2.8 million and the opportunity to buy these extremely valuable twenty-five thousand acres, including the Mahoning Mine near Hibbing, was lost. As Dad said, "Gates did not want to buy the land, he wanted to steal it."

After the foreclosure by Rockefeller, Grandfather said that his general manager of the DM&N Railroad, Donald Philbin, would occasionally get drunk at the Spalding Hotel in Duluth after the trial, and "curse and damn" Rockefeller. Grandfather appreciated his loyalty to the Merrritts but told him that he now worked for Rockefeller and if he kept berating Rockefeller he would soon be out of a job. He convinced Philbin to go to St. Paul and "camp on Jim Hill's doorstep" until Hill pursued buying the twenty-five thousand acres held by Wright and Davis on the Mesabi. Philbin apparently followed Alfred's advice because he was hired by Hill and spent the rest of his career working for the Hill interests on the Range. After three months Hill agreed to look into the possibility and sent his son to check it out. Hill's son Louis saw the opportunity and spent much of the next three years living at the Spalding Hotel in Duluth. In 1899 James J. Hill of Great Northern Railway fame bought what turned out to be perhaps the single most valuable iron ore deposits on the Mesabi Range for $4,050,000.[21]

Thus Hill and the Great Northern Railway were on the Mesabi

Range providing competition to U. S. Steel, which bought the Rockefeller interests. If Rockefeller had purchased the Wright and Davis lands this competing rail line would never have happened, and Hill would not have had the enormous profits for the Great Northern Ore Company to which he transferred these ore bodies.

"What Rockefeller Did to Us"

On February 18 and 25, 1912, the *New York World* magazine published a two-installment description by my father's older sister, Alta Merritt, under the name Hepziabeth Merritt, of what it was like growing up in the Merritt family with the cloud of what Rockefeller had done to the "Merritt boys" hanging over them.

She told how as a young girl she came to fear Rockefeller. She vividly told how her father and Uncle Lon would not talk about Rockefeller when she asked about what went on, yet as she grew up she would so often hear neighbors, friends, and visitors say, as she came into a room, "There is Alf Merritt's girl. It's a shame what Rockefeller did to the Merritt boys!" When she was very young she attended her Uncle Cassius's funeral and recalled how afterward she heard her father and Uncle Lon talk about how bad they felt about his death, which they attributed to Rockefeller. She heard them say "over and over again," "Oh, if only we had never heard of him!" And she knew that "him" was John D. Rockefeller. "Those were sad, sad days in our family. It was all quite too much for my little head to fathom."[22]

Alta wrote that when she and other family members reached higher grades in school others would point them out and talk of them "in tones of pity and compassion. We always found a way to let those who were pitying us know that we didn't want any pity at all, that we didn't care a thing about Rockefeller or any one else, and that father was just the greatest man that ever lived, anyhow."

Summing up, Alta listed the things Rockefeller brought upon the Merritts: "The death of my Uncle Cassius. Years of sorrow and worry brought to my Grandmother and all the family. The taking away from my father and his brothers the financial reward to which they were entitled for all their efforts. The white hairs brought too soon to the heads of both my father and mother. The days and years of gloom, of trouble, of worry brought into the lives of children who had a right to happiness. Perhaps it doesn't mean much to others—to me it always has seemed a bitter burden that we ought not to have had to bear. Never before have I dared write the name Rockefeller as often as I have here. And even now I am a little bit afraid."[23]

Author Don W. Larson, in his book *Land of the Giants*, concludes that Gates "slyly stole the mines and railroad from the Merritts."[24] After I read this I called Larson, who had never interviewed any Merritts. I asked him how he got the story right when so many prominent authors failed to do so. He said he had reviewed records at the Minnesota Historical Society. He told me, "It became obvious what had happened, so I said so in my book."

There is no doubt in my mind that if Gates and Rockefeller had been honest in dealing with the Merritts, Rockefeller could have made far more money than the $60 million he was paid for the Merritt properties when they were turned into the Steel Trust in 1901.

In doing the research for this book, I was able to confirm what my father told me all my life—that the Merritts were poorly served by two lawyers in whom they had placed great trust—Joseph B. Cotton, who was their counsel for several years during the organization of their mining companies and the railroad, and A. A. Harris, who was chief counsel in the lawsuit against John D. Rockefeller.

Immediately after Rockefeller foreclosed on the Merritts, and they lost everything in February 1894, Joseph Cotton asked Grandfather on bended knee to be released from any further obligations, telling them he had been offered a five-year contract to serve as Rockefeller's lawyer in Duluth. Alfred agreed to his request, which was most unfortunate because Cotton immediately became an active participant in defending Rockefeller against the lawsuit in federal court and Rockefeller became privy to considerable confidential information.

A. A. Harris had to be sued, following the federal court action, to return stock he held in escrow, having reneged on his promise to return the stock upon full payment of his legal fees, which had been settled. He also refused to return the Merritts' files and engaged in other unseemly intimidation. Subsequently Harris had to be cited for contempt of court before he would comply with the decision against him obtained by Alfred.[25]

It is interesting to note that in subsequent years the four largest of the Merritt ore properties, the Mountain Iron, Missabe Mountain in Virginia, the Biwabik, and the Adams, produced at least 214 million tons of high-grade hematite iron ore. By comparison, the Michigan mines put into the Consolidated by Rockefeller—the Aurora and Penokee-Gogebic—produced at the most 10 million tons. As far as is known, the Rockefeller mine in Cuba never produced any iron ore.

It has been frustrating for me and others of our clan to read in books and articles about the Merritts and the Mesabi that the loss of their enormous holdings on the Mesabi, as well as the railroad, was due to their becoming overextended and that the financial "genius" of Rockefeller was their undoing. Some authors would throw in the huge economic depression of 1893. There is some truth in all of those factors, no doubt, but the greater truth is that Gates and Rockefeller did not play fair with the Merritts. An honest Rockefeller could have made a billion dollars off the Mesabi Range and his son would have become the King of Iron. Rockefeller sold these properties for $60 million to J. Pierpont Morgan to join U.S. Steel in 1901. The sale of Consolidated stock "swelled Rockefeller's net worth beyond $200 million with a $55 million profit."[26]

Several other books have explored my family's fleecing. The most scholarly is the 1979 book *Iron Frontier*, by David A. Walker, published by the Minnesota Historical Society. Walker did not conclude that the Merritts were defrauded by Rockefeller. He told me after the book was published that he had an opinion on the subject but could not find written documentation. Perhaps now he could make his opinion public based on Chernow's discovery of the letters between Gates and Frank Rockefeller.

A leading history of Minnesota displays a lack of understanding about what really happened back in those days on the Mesabi.

Theodore Blegen wrote that the wheels of a heavy wagon cut down in the soil to a red powdery substance from which the captain of the Merritt crew gathered up a fifty-pound pack and took it to Duluth to have it tested.[27] Blegen misstated the account of the discovery in *Seven Iron Men*, by Paul de Kruif, who reported in his book that earlier in 1890, before the discovery at Mountain Iron, the Merritts had observed red powdery soil that they thought was iron, but they were doubtful and still looked for a vein of ore.

The discovery occurred when the crew dug a test pit fifteen feet down at Mountain Iron and, as described by the Minnesota Geological Survey at that time, the Merritts' crew under direction of Captain J. A. Nichols "encountered soft hematite which was the first body of soft ore discovered on the Mesabi." It was from that discovery at Mountain Iron that a fifty-pound sack of the soft hematite was brought to Duluth, where it was analyzed at 64 percent iron ore. The idea of Blegen's that the discovery was from wagon wheels sinking in the powdery soil was repeated recently in a book published by the Minnesota Historical Society called *A Popular History of Minnesota*.[28] The author, Norman Risjord, a retired professor from Madison, Wisconsin, should have read David Walker's *Iron Frontier*, which attributes the discovery on November 16, 1890, to the same test pit at Mountain Iron as reported by de Kruif in *Seven Iron Men*.

Risjord also claims that the Merritts "exulted in high living, splashing money all over Duluth, but they proved to be backwoodsmen when they ran up against the fiscal genie employed by John D. Rockefeller."[29] This allegation is baseless, because there is no evidence supporting such a claim. Indeed, immediately after the discovery, the Merritts plunged into arranging transportation as discussed earlier; arguing with doubting geologists who discounted the rich Mesabi ore because it would be mined, for the first time in the world, with steam shovels. They also were engaged in building the first railroad from the Mesabi to Duluth and constructing the world's largest ore dock. They had no time for "high living."

Marvin Lamppa, in his good book, *Minnesota's Iron Country*, looks at the discovery and development of Minnesota's three iron ranges. Lamppa takes the financial entanglements among the Merritts,

With my mother and sister at Tischer Creek in the Hunter's Park neighborhood of Duluth in 1939, when I was five years old.

Rockefeller, and his cohorts right up to the litigation and then stops short of the fraud proved in federal district court.[30] The only books on the ending of the Merritts' time on the Mesabi that either come close to the truth or nail it are *Titan* by Chernow and Larson's *Land of the Giants*.

Grandfather made enough money out of the settlement, after paying off all creditors, to go out west and continue mining. He mined lead and silver in the Moscow, Idaho, area and developed the Cave Canyon Mine near Barstow, California. At a Union Pacific branch line near that mine, President E. H. Harriman "came into contact with the genius whose personal achievement it had been to assemble the Minnesota ore lands," namely, Alfred Merritt. The

Wall Street Journal went on to quote Grandfather urging Harriman to "establish your own furnaces, make your own rails." Harriman was unhappy with his rail supply, and the two men conferred at the wilderness way station. They commenced to do business with Alfred Merritt either selling or optioning the Cave Canyon iron ore mine to Harriman. During 1902–10, while this mine was being developed, the Alfred Merritt family lived in a large home on Colorado Street in Pasadena with an orange grove behind the house.

Some years after the litigation against Rockefeller, after he moved back to Duluth, Alfred Merritt talked things over with J. L. Washburn. About Rockefeller, Washburn said, "If hell was an amphitheater, and it got hotter as you got closer to the stage, John D. Rockefeller would be in the front row."[31]

My Early Years in Duluth

I was told, early in my life, the stories of my family's history on the Iron Range. By the time I had reached the eighth grade, I had read Paul de Kruif's *Seven Iron Men*, and I knew well how deep my family's roots ran in Duluth. My family lived in the Hunter's Park neighborhood in northeast Duluth, two blocks from Washburn Grade School, which I attended through sixth grade. The landscape there was wide; it was urban but had plenty of open space for pickup sports. For a short time I had a trapline not far from our home on Columbus Avenue. I was interested in cowboy music, especially Gene Autry. When we heard he was coming to town with his horse, Champion, who would be staying in the barn owned by the parents of my classmate Judy MacGregor, we naturally trooped to the barn to see Champion. That was an event to remember. In addition to listening to Gene Autry sing "Deep in the Heart of Texas," I listened in the morning before school quite often to a local country-western singer "Famous Lashaway" and remember liking his rendition of "Don't Fence Me In."

As early as 1944, while a sixth grader, I began politicking. I mounted numerous Franklin Roosevelt buttons on a blue pennant, which I still have, and hung it in a front window of our home during

Outside North Star Timber Company barracks in northeastern Minnesota during the summer of 1951.

FDR's fourth-term election campaign that fall. My dad had been active in politics in the late 1920s and 1930s as a supporter of, first, Al Smith and then FDR for president. He was a delegate to the state and national Democratic Party Conventions of 1932. In March 1933 he attended FDR's first inauguration and in 1933 was appointed postmaster in Duluth. Stories of those days were common at home. Pictures and memorabilia of Roosevelt were prevalent both at home and at Dad's corner office in the Federal Building, located in what is now the Duluth Civic Center Historic District.

During junior high in the 1940s, I spent three and a half years as a *Duluth News Tribune* carrier, trekking around Hunter's Park in the early hours or delivering newspapers from my bike in the summer months. That morning paper route taught me many lessons, especially how to run a business. In the 1940s that meant collecting from

Eleanor Roosevelt addresses our student group at the United Nations
in New York in 1953. I'm in the light sport coat just to the right of Mrs.
Roosevelt.

customers in person and then delivering the proceeds to the downtown newspaper offices. I recall earning about six dollars a week.

I graduated in 1951 from Central High School in Duluth. I was impressed with the commencement speech by Laurence Gould, the
president of Carleton College in Northfield, Minnesota. Mr. Gould
was second in command on Richard E. Byrd's first trip in 1929–30
to the Antarctic. His speech outlined good values for us to follow
through life.

Entering the University of Minnesota Duluth (UMD) in the fall
of 1951 at the height of the Korean War, I majored in political science with a double minor in business and economics and Air Force
ROTC. My four years of ROTC gave me an excellent education in

leadership. We had training on the drill field and a tough month of summer camp at Ellsworth Air Force Base in South Dakota, and we were required to prepare lesson plans and teach our fellow classmates. One such assignment of mine in the fall of 1954, around the time of the Battle of Dien Bien Phu, during the First Indochina War, was to lecture on the South Vietnamese leader Ngo Diem and the dramatic defeat suffered by the French at the hands of the Vietnamese. Nearly ten years later, after I was out of the air force, my outfit, the 507th Tactical Control Group, participated in the overthrow of the Diem regime on orders from Washington.

In 1970 I attended a reunion of my college fraternity, Beta Phi Kappa, in Duluth. One of my ROTC classmates, aviator Dave Everson, was in a Hanoi prison at the time, having been shot down by the Viet Cong. His wife attended our reunion at Paulucci Hall and spoke. Afterward, I talked to an ROTC instructor from UMD about the irony that I had to study about South Vietnam, then still called Indochina, during my ROTC days and that my outfit had been part of the overthrow of Ngo Diem, which resulted in his death. I said the air force either was very prescient about a coming war or had something to do with getting involved in the Vietnam War. His answer was "a little of both."

In February 1953, I traveled to New York and Washington, D.C., for a student group introduction to the United Nations and the federal government. There were about thirty of us from around the country. We watched the United Nations in action and met with Eleanor Roosevelt. I had my picture taken with her. In Washington I visited with Senator Hubert Humphrey outside the Senate Chambers, and our group heard from Senators Robert Taft of Ohio, Wayne Morse of Oregon, and Herbert Lehman of New York.

I became active in a unique group of students from both major parties at UMD, the Democratic–Republican Forum, which sponsored speeches on campus from former Minnesota governor Harold Stassen, U.S. Senator Hubert Humphrey, former California governor Earl Warren, U.S. Representative James Roosevelt, and U.S. Representative John Blatnik. I joined the Young Democratic-Farmer-Labor Party (YDFL) and was elected Eighth Congressional

District chairman in 1953. As a result, I was invited to talk politics in the home of a Duluth lawyer, Gerald Heaney, whom I encountered often afterward. He became a regent of the University of Minnesota in the 1960s and was appointed to the Eighth Circuit Court of Appeals by President Lyndon Johnson in 1966.

In 1954 I attended a state convention in the Twin Cities of the YDFL party, where Senator Estes Kefauver of Tennessee spoke in his trademark coonskin cap as a candidate for president. During these YDFL days I became acquainted with Wayne Olson and Ron Anderson, both of whom became state chairs of the YDFL and later attained statewide offices in Minnesota government—Wayne as commissioner of the Department of Conservation and Ron as a member of the Railroad and Warehouse Commission.

During the fall of 1954, Hubert Humphrey was campaigning for reelection in the Duluth area and was scheduled to speak at UMD. As president of the student council, I went to meet him at the Spalding Hotel and escort him to the campus. When I arrived at the eighth floor of the hotel, Governor Orville Freeman, Congressman Blatnik, and Gerald Heaney—then national committeeman for the DFL Party—were all in the hotel suite and told me to go into the bedroom where Senator Humphrey was stretched out in bed sick. He quickly told me that if I would go across Superior Street to the Boyce Drug Store and fill the prescription that he wrote out for me, then he could probably make the appointed speech. He said to tell the druggist that Humphrey was a pharmacist. "Don't take no for an answer!" he said. So I dutifully went to the drug store and argued with the druggist to get whatever it was that Humphrey wanted, paid a dollar (which, of course, I never got back), returned to the hotel, and accompanied Humphrey to the campus, where I introduced him to the assembly. I recall two more events from that day: first, Humphrey reached out to a Republican student on the stage, Jim Maher, spending more time talking about him than the Democrat on the stage. Second, after the speech, which was well delivered by the ill Humphrey (I wonder what was in that prescription), we drove back down to the Spalding Hotel. During the drive, where I was seated next to Hubert in the front seat, he unleashed memorable profanity. He was upset about a statement by President Eisenhower's Secretary of Defense, Charlie Wilson, former CEO of General Motors who was quoted in the press as saying, "What's good for General Motors is good for the country!" What Wilson actually said was, "What's good for the country is good for General Motors, and vice versa."

During my year as president of the student council at UMD we reformed that body and were able to persuade the provost, Raymond Darland, that we should join the National Student Association. Dr. Darland questioned whether that was a good idea because he was afraid that the NSA was a pink outfit, meaning, tainted with Communists. I assured him that we had checked it out and it was not. Ironically, several years later it was revealed that the CIA had infiltrated the NSA.

In the spring of 1955 I graduated from UMD and was commissioned as a second lieutenant in the air force. Before serving on active duty, I spent a year and a half in graduate school at the University of Minnesota's Public Administration Center in Minneapolis, now the Humphrey School of Public Affairs. Professor Walter Heller was my teacher in two courses, public finance and fiscal policy. I wrote a master's plan B paper, "Taxation of Iron Ore in Minnesota," under his supervision. He also served on my orals panel for the degree. Heller was a superb teacher in these seminar courses, inviting us to his home on several occasions. He later served both John Kennedy and Lyndon Johnson as chairman of the Council of Economic Advisers from 1961 to 1965. I kept in touch with him after graduating and regard him as the most influential of many excellent teachers I had over the years.

During my first year in graduate school I was a research assistant and spent the year working part-time researching and writing an administrative history of the Children's Bureau of the Minnesota Department of Welfare. This involved interviewing state officials such as Welfare Department Deputy Commissioner Ray Lappegard, who later served the Wendell Anderson administration as commissioner of highways. My fellow research colleagues on the Welfare Department project were Bert Silver and Bob Atwell, both of whom

Receiving the Provost Medal as an air force cadet commander in June 1955 from University of Minnesota Duluth provost Ray Darland.

went on to distinguished careers in public service—Bert as a high official in the Departments of Commerce and Civil Rights in Washington, D.C., and Bob as president of Pitzer College in Claremont, California, and then president of the American Council on Education in Washington, D.C.

My air force active service began in Victoria, Texas, at Foster Air Force Base, situated between Houston and Corpus Christi, not far from Port Lavaca on the Gulf of Mexico. At Foster I was an intelligence officer, and an early task was to create a motto for the 512th Tactical Control Group. I came up with "Knowledge Before Action," which I thought summed up the mission of a radar outfit controlling tactical aircraft. This motto has been relevant to many of my endeavors since then, far beyond radar and aircraft. In May

23

1957, I was transferred to Shaw Air Force Base in Sumter, South Carolina. My job at Shaw was as installations engineer with related assignments throughout the southeastern states, where I monitored radio relay sites. The unit was the 507th Tactical Control Group, Ninth Air Force.

Having been a golfer since I was twelve and winning a letter for golf at Central High School, I played golf at the course we had at Shaw Air Force Base. In the spring of 1958, I read in our base newspaper that if I wore my uniform I could gain free entry to see the Masters Golf Tournament at Augusta, Georgia. I decided to put on my first lieutenant summer uniform and drive over to Augusta on the final day of play. I drove down Magnolia Lane and parked near the beautiful white clubhouse. I walked out to the tenth hole, where my hero Ben Hogan was hitting his second shot to the green. At noon I went into the clubhouse locker room and saw Gene Sarazen standing by himself looking a bit lonely. He had been famous for winning several major tournaments beginning with the U.S. Open in 1922 and the 1935 Masters at Augusta with an incredible double eagle on the fifteenth hole. I went over and introduced myself and asked him if he would wait while I ran out to my car and brought back my copy of the Herbert Warren Wind book *The Story of American Golf,* which has a chapter about Gene Sarazen. He waited and I have treasured ever since his kind autograph. I went back to following Ben Hogan awhile but switched to a young player named Arnold Palmer, who was challenging the leader Ken Venturi. I saw Palmer win his first major tournament. After that I waited outside the clubhouse and watched Bobby Jones slip a green jacket on Arnie Palmer. On my return that night I relived these fond memories and thought about how the course was filled with beautiful azaleas.

I was married late that summer in Duluth to Marilyn Pederson. I had met her while at UMD, roller-skating at the Duluth Curling Club. We honeymooned on the North Shore and then headed to South Carolina, stopping for two days at Fontana Village in the Smoky Mountains. After my air force days were over, she worked for the University of Minnesota near the law school where I pursued my law degree.

Because of my graduate work in public administration and my air force experience, I interviewed in Washington, D.C., for a job with the U.S. Department of Labor and with McKinsey & Company as a management intern. I received favorable responses from them and also inquired about working for General Mills in Minneapolis. Marilyn's aunt Annabelle Johnson was General Mills president James Ford Bell's private secretary. I interviewed with him in September 1958. Annabelle wrote after the meeting that Mr. Bell was favorably impressed and told one of his employees to contact me, which he did.

If I had pursued that prospect, or the others in Washington, D.C., my subsequent career would have been markedly different. Instead of those opportunities, I enrolled at the University of Minnesota Law School, graduating in 1962. As a beginning lawyer with the Minneapolis firm Mackall Crounse & Moore in the summer of 1962, I was a general practitioner for the first two years and then for the next seven years I specialized in motor carrier law. This practice meant a lot of contested administrative hearings and brief writing for trucking companies either seeking operating authority for their firms or protesting other carriers seeking to operate over routes they already served. This regulated field was begun in the early 1930s in Minnesota for intrastate commerce and by the Motor Carrier Act passed by Congress in 1935 for interstate commerce. I traveled a great deal for hearings around the country for those cases, which became a good foundation for my future work in the environmental field.

My first appellate case was in November 1964, just two years after starting practice. It was a pro bono assignment prompted by the Minnesota Supreme Court's need for lawyers to handle cases on appeal by indigent defendants. I represented Muller Taylor, who had been convicted of serious sex crimes in Hennepin County District Court. In reviewing the facts and transcript of his trial, I determined that there were four constitutional issues. Police had detained Taylor for 41 hours without the benefit of counsel and interrogated him without counsel present, resulting in damaging admissions. I spent 212 hours writing the brief, preparing for the argument in the Supreme Court and reading all the relevant Supreme Court decisions on the rights of the accused. I went over to the University of Minnesota Law School to enlist the help of my criminal law professor, Yale Kamisar, who was a nationally known expert on the rights of the accused.

The oral argument went very well—Justice Robert Sheran had read the briefs and cases, so we had a great back-and-forth discussion, just like in law school. The court hammered the assistant county attorney hard, and when we finished Chief Justice Oscar Knutson commended me on my presentation—win or lose. A law clerk introduced himself and also said I did a good job but that I was going to lose because my client had such a bad previous criminal record.

He was right. Justice Sheran wrote the opinion complimenting my brief as "perceptive and scholarly," which I appreciated. Because Taylor was to be released from Stillwater prison just three months after the decision, there was no time to appeal to the U.S. Supreme Court. That was unfortunate because the U.S. Supreme Court likely would have reversed the Minnesota Supreme Court based on the violation of Taylor's constitutional rights.

Entering Politics in the Sixties

By 1966 I was beginning to think seriously about activity in the Democratic-Farmer-Labor Party, but fortunately I did not participate in the intraparty battle that year, when the DFL lieutenant governor, Sandy Keith, tried to unseat DFL governor Karl Rolvaag. I did side with Rolvaag at the precinct caucus and voted for him in the primary, which he won against the endorsed Keith, but Rolvaag lost to the Republican candidate, Harold LeVander, in the general election.

In 1967 I began a long stretch of vigorous activity in the DFL. I became ward club chairman of New Hope, the community in northwestern Hennepin County where I still live today. Our DFL ward club held a debate on the Vietnam War in January 1968 at Cooper High School with two high-profile debaters and drew a very large

With my father, Glen J. Merritt, in 1966, viewing the compass used by George Stuntz while he surveyed northeastern Minnesota in the mid-1800s.

crowd. One of our members, Bob Watkins, wrote a long white paper against the war, which convinced me to oppose it.

I was also a delegate to the 1968 DFL state convention in June at the Hilton Hotel in downtown St. Paul. As a delegate I was the Humphrey leader on the platform committee and helped draft a platform plank on the Vietnam War. It was the product of a sub-committee composed of equal numbers of McCarthy and Humphrey delegates that included Professor Leo Hurwicz of the University of Minnesota. Hurwicz was a McCarthy delegate, and it was a pleasure to work with him drafting the Vietnam plank. Shortly before he died in 2008 he was awarded the Nobel Prize in economics for his pioneering work on economics.

NEW HOPE DFL chairman, Grant Merritt, left, and Lee Erhard, right, joined with other DFL ward clubs recently in supporting a boycott of Red Owl stores by picketing and distributing literature at the New Hope shopping center in an effort to induce Red Owl stores to stop purchasing grapes from California table grape growers. Mrs. Myles Winjum, 3841 Gettysburg ave. receives a leaflet from Erhard.

Boycotting Red Owl stores during Cesar Chavez's grape boycott in December 1968.

The plank was adopted by the full committee. It called for a coalition government in Vietnam and withdrawal of thirty-five thousand troops. Unfortunately, the Humphrey camp at the state convention forced us to withdraw the compromise we had forged with the Eugene McCarthy supporters. The morning after we reached agreement on this compromise plank, I was called to the top floor of the Hilton Hotel, where former ambassador Eugenia Anderson told me, "The eyes of Hanoi were on this convention" and the "Paris Peace Talks" were at such a delicate stage that we could not afford to pass our compromise plank. That made me wonder, who was I, a lowly ward club chairman from a small suburb, to question the vice president of the United States? So I went along.

I have always believed that if Humphrey had accepted that plank he would have been elected president. I also learned that if I was positive an adopted position on an issue was right, I should stick to the position, even if subjected to pressure. That lesson came into play right after the meeting with the ambassador.

Our platform committee also approved a plank I drafted on practices of the Reserve Mining Company in Silver Bay, an issue I had begun working on in the fall of 1967. The plank stated that "the use of Lake Superior as a dumping ground for mining or industrial wastes must be prohibited." Robert Bartlett in his book *The Reserve Mining Controversy* says adoption of this plank by the state central committee marked "a turning point in state politics—the first time a Minnesota political party had gone on record opposing the disposal of tailings in Lake Superior."[32]

The morning after my session with the ambassador, I was summoned to Congressman Blatnik's suite, where the congressman admonished me for the Reserve Mining plank we had adopted the night before, calling for an end to the company's dumping of sixty-seven thousand tons of tailings a day into Lake Superior. Blatnik, who represented Reserve's district, said, "I want that plank out of there." I refused to back down and the plank became part of the 1968 state DFL Party platform.

I attended the National Democratic Convention in late August 1968 in Chicago, where I witnessed the huge demonstrations outside the convention hall; Mayor Richard Daley had Chicago police on the scene and the National Guard was summoned to deal with outbursts of violence. Peace rallies were in full force with a candlelight parade, which I observed from a window in the Hilton Hotel on Michigan Avenue. I came away with lots of stories to tell back home. I was there only as an observer, but thanks to several friends I was an alternate delegate for a day, and a delegate for an hour. From a good vantage point across from the rostrum, I saw many of the well-known newsmen and delegates, such as actors Paul Newman and Shirley MacLaine. I could hear them talking to each other right below me on the convention floor. I met Jim Farley, postmaster general from the FDR era, and Martin Agronsky, a favorite radio commentator. My dad and I had listened to him on the radio each morning at seven when I came back from delivering the *Duluth News Tribune* in the 1940s.

The convention business on Wednesday dragged on until about two o'clock Thursday morning. I was back on Michigan Avenue at about three o'clock following a major outburst of violence. A Gene McCarthy supporter saw my Humphrey buttons as we stood on the street and suggested that I should leave. I heeded his advice. After returning home I wrote up my convention experience for the local newspaper in New Hope, which concluded:

> As I evaluate the week's experience, I recall my 6th grade teacher's admonition to her students—"I must learn to respect the rights of others by practicing greater self-control." If the demonstrators and police alike had followed this good advice, the sad events of Chicago would never have happened.

ENVIRONMENTALISM
AND THE RESERVE
MINING CONTROVERSY

What Is Being Dumped in Lake Superior?

During the summer of 1955, after graduating from college, I worked for a contractor in Silver Bay, Minnesota, on the north shore of Lake Superior, digging trenches in the clay and helping polish the floors at the high school before it opened that fall. I would stay during the week with my uncle Milton and his wife, Jean, at one of their cabins along the East Beaver Bay shoreline below the Mattson Store run by Milton. Milton's brother Kermit was working for one of the contractors when he wasn't fishing commercially.[1] At that time, the dumping of waste slag directly into the lake, which would begin in the spring of 1956, didn't capture my interest.

It wasn't for another twelve years that I would recognize the threat to Lake Superior from the Reserve Mining pollution. My involvement began when Milton and Jean arrived at our home on November 5, 1967, for a visit. It was not an ordinary family get-together. Milton clearly had a purpose in mind. He was getting information from a number of sources that in addition to taconite tailings, chemicals, oils, and other pollutants were being dumped into the lake as well. Milton began telling me about the "hoodwinking" of the public by Reserve Mining. He made the following points, which I recorded in my journal that evening:

31

- "Tailings" or slag were being dumped every day directly into the lake.
- Waste oil was being pumped through the two chutes into the lake—thousands of gallons per month.
- Waste chemicals and acids were also being dumped in the lake.
- Two carloads per day of fly ash were also going down the chutes to the lake.[2]

The slag and waste dump was growing. For example, Milton said, fly ash had formerly been disposed of in the woods behind the plant. Now it went into the lake.

My journal went on: "The slag and pollution can be seen in the water as far west as Two Harbors. It collects on the bottom and kills fish eggs in spawning grounds. Milton says it goes across to the south shore as well. Reserve Mining has been hoodwinking the public recently, since the newspaper publicity, Milton said. For instance, it has called the picture of the slag in the Sunday *Minneapolis Tribune* an 'illusion.' Second, when Reserve heard that Secretary of the Interior Udall was going to fly over the delta and plant buildings, they 'seeded' the slag with grass seed—thus temporarily turning the area green—now, of course, it is back to the dirty brown.[3]

I was now hooked on doing something to stop Reserve's egregious pollution of Lake Superior. My journal entry concludes: "The only way to force Reserve is to apply political pressure. Milton tells me Reserve is doing nothing to solve it, when obviously something could be done."

Early November 1967 marked the beginning of a new chapter in my life—as a citizen environmental activist. I made a decision that profoundly affected my life, my career, and my family. Of course, I did not foresee all the changes that would result, but I was absolutely committed to stopping the dumping of tailings by Reserve Mining.

I devised a plan. I would organize opposition from the New Hope Democratic-Farmer-Labor Club, which I chaired. We would seek publicity, write key party officeholders, and ask the state environmental agency to take action. DFL State Party Chairman Warren Spannaus appointed me cochair of the state DFL preplatform committee, and we held hearings around the state to draft the proposed state platform for the 1968 state convention. One of the planks we developed was the one later adopted by the state DFL and quoted in chapter 1, calling for an end to the Reserve dumping.[4]

I had been fascinated by politics from my earliest days. So it was quite natural that, after hearing the details from my uncle Milton Mattson regarding Reserve's massive insult to Lake Superior, I would think the solution must involve political action. The political overtones of my decision would soon draw me deeper into politics for better or worse. I couldn't have foreseen the tangle of controversies, intrigue, setbacks, the many victories and defeats that would grow from my new course.

Opposition to the dumping of taconite tailings in Lake Superior can be traced to the original state of Minnesota hearings in 1947 on the permits sought by the Reserve Mining Company's predecessor, Oglebay Norton. The hearings, held by the Minnesota Department of Conservation and the Water Pollution Control Commission, took place in Duluth and in St. Paul and were chaired by the commissioner of the Conservation Department, Chester A. Wilson, a lawyer from Stillwater. Reserve chose to build most of its taconite-processing operations at a location east of Beaver Bay on the shores of Lake Superior. Their plan was to use the lake for discharge of what they claimed was "mere sand" through two gigantic "launder chutes."

Representatives from early conservation groups in Duluth like United Northern Sportsmen and the Brotherhood of Railway Trainmen spoke out against the proposed discharge, as did several commercial fishermen. They testified that the tailings would interfere with the fish along the shore. The trainmen's union introduced a letter stating that "the silt from the tailings will never settle. . . . You can have a glass full from any Duluth faucet in about four years from now if this project goes through."[5]

University of Minnesota professor E. W. Davis worked for twenty-five years to develop the process of beneficiating taconite into pellets for the blast furnaces. Twenty years later, in his book *Pioneering with Taconite,* Davis referred to these 1947 permit hearings: "It became obvious that the opposition was trying to . . . delay the construction of a taconite plant on the lake shore. Why they were doing this was never clear to me." A Minnesota Department of Conservation official was less mystified than Davis. He said the department looked into who was behind the opposition and claimed "it was the Communists."[6]

Company lawyer William K. Montague of Duluth ridiculed the opponents. He introduced results from a physical model of what would allegedly happen to the tailings entering the lake. This model was built by several University of Minnesota employees at the Mines Experiment Station in Minneapolis. It contained a tailings chute, tailings, and water for the tailings to enter. The idea was that the tailings would all sink to the bottom of the deep chasm off Silver Bay in a "great density current" created by the tailings hitting the lake waters. The only problem was the water temperature in this model was the room temperature of seventy-two degrees. That meant that the viscosity of the water was far different from the year-round average temperature of Lake Superior's water off Silver Bay, approximately forty degrees. Tailings entering lake water at that temperature are far less likely to head for the bottom of the so-called great density current. These important temperature differences were not made to the public officials.[7]

A second problem with the model was that its tailings were not nearly as fine as the actual tailings would be, making them heavier and more likely to head for the bottom. Unfortunately, neither of these problems was explored by any of the government or citizen participants in these hearings. After some eight public sessions, the state agencies drafted permits for the Silver Bay operation that included appropriation of Lake Superior waters for the operation and a discharge permit. The latter provided what should have been a good triggering mechanism to withdraw the permit after the operation was begun in 1955. The permit required confining the tailings to a nine-square-mile zone off Silver Bay, three by three by three miles. "The tailings were not to include any material quantities of matter soluble in water. The tailings were to have no material adverse effects on fish. The tailings were not to cause any material unlawful pollution of Lake Superior. The tailings were to have no material adverse effects on public water supplies." Finally, the permit provided for revocation if any of the conditions were violated.[8]

By the 1960s it was increasingly evident to North Shore commercial fishermen, as well as onlookers or tourists, that the tailings were now spreading well beyond the nine-square-mile zone off Silver Bay. On many days it was easy to see the green water all along the shore toward Two Harbors as well as out in the open water of the lake toward Wisconsin. The verbal and written citizens' objections were ignored by the state agencies and denied by the company. Specific citizen complaints were subjected to obfuscation by Ed Schmid, Reserve spokesman, who alternately called the green water an "illusion" or a "natural phenomenon," without acknowledging the inherent contradiction in those descriptions.

When Mrs. Edel Schneiderhorn called Ed Schmid over to her home, perched above East Beaver Bay about two miles west of the Silver Bay plant, she showed Schmid what she believed were fine dust tailings blown over from the plant. Mr. Schmid attempted to dismiss any company involvement by telling her that those particles were from the ore boats passing by. Edel was not amused, pointing out it was February and there hadn't been any ore boats since December.

Until Milton Mattson, Edel's brother, began to voice objections and alerted me to the problem in November 1967, complaints were mounting but there was no organized opposition. Probably the first organized effort was the DFL Party platform of 1968 and the platform committee action leading up to that adoption in the form of several hearings around the state during the spring of 1968. After the hearing we held in Duluth that spring I was interviewed for the first time about the Reserve dumping by WDIO-TV. This interview took place the year before Cleveland's Cuyahoga River caught fire, an event that added to the growing interest in the social and economic cost of pollution.

In November 1968 I wrote a letter to Charles Stoddard, regional

35

coordinator for Interior Secretary Stewart Udall at the request of Milton Mattson. Milton was concerned that the multiagency study headed by Stoddard was not as accurate as it could be because the study had sampled Reserve's tailings during the summer of 1968, when half the plant was shut down.

After sending this letter to Stoddard I forwarded a copy to Jim Shoop before leaving on a trip to Los Angeles for a hearing on one of my trucking cases. A reporter with the *Minneapolis Star,* Shoop had asked me at the 1968 Democratic National Convention in Chicago to let him know if there was something newsworthy on the Reserve Mining case. Shoop wrote a story based on my letter, and upon my return home I had a call from John Pegors, who identified himself as a member of the Minnesota Environmental Control Citizens Association (MECCA), which I had never heard of. He invited me to a meeting of its board of directors at the St. Paul Area Council of Churches building.

I entered a small conference room and encountered a discussion about the pollution of Pig's Eye Island by a group seated around a table with an energized guy at the end with an upside-down pipe bobbing in his mouth as he talked. This was Larry Cohen, later mayor of St. Paul and a district judge in Ramsey County. Near the other end of the table was a white-haired man named Steve Gadler, whom I later learned was a board member at the Minnesota Pollution Control Agency. John Pegors introduced me. I was given a seat in the corner, told this was the board of the Minnesota Environmental Control Citizens Association, and listened to their discussion of the pollution threat to Pig's Eye. This was a mystery to me, since I lived way across the Twin Cities metropolitan area in New Hope and practiced law in downtown Minneapolis. I had never heard of Pig's Eye. The discussion focused on pollution from the North Star Steel plant on the island named Pig's Eye, which was adjacent to homes in St. Paul. It wasn't long after that meeting that MECCA invited me to join the board and head up a new task force named after Lake Superior. I agreed. This made MECCA the first environmental group to fight head-on Reserve Mining's daily dumping of 67,000 tons of taconite tailings in Lake Superior.

I decided that this was an opportunity to help save this greatest of all lakes and that I could help lead the fight. My idea was to educate people about the problem, arouse public opinion, and then take action through the political and administrative process. I didn't have a university degree in political science and advanced degrees in public administration and law for nothing. I was able to take on this battle for several other reasons. First of all, I loved Lake Superior, having grown up in Duluth and spent many hours in the state parks all along the North Shore as well as with relatives along the lake in Beaver Bay, Grand Marais, and Hovland. Second, I had a rather unique law practice as a motor carrier lawyer with the firm of Mackall Crounse & Moore, which enabled me to put in a considerable number of billable hours at hearings and writing briefs in the then-heavily regulated trucking business. This allowed me to take off more time than would otherwise be possible to pursue work on the Reserve Mining case. Also, I sensed not only that this was a battle worth pursuing but also that it was one we could win. I am sure ego was also involved, but the greater motivation for me was to organize opposition to stop the pollution of Lake Superior.

The Stoddard Report

In early January 1969 reporter Ron Way, in covering the environment for the *Minneapolis Tribune,* got a scoop on the release of the five-federal-agency study of the Reserve discharge headed by Charles Stoddard. The study was completed and sent by Stoddard to the Interior Department in Washington, D.C. It concluded that the Reserve permit was being violated, that the tailings were causing harm to the lake biota and fishery. The study also found that the tailings from Silver Bay were being transported into Wisconsin waters and toward Duluth. Furthermore, they were causing material discoloration of Lake Superior waters.

This study, soon known as the Stoddard Report, was infuriating to Reserve, and its corporate owners, Republic and Armco Steel Corporations. They all swung into action to discredit the report. Congressman John Blatnik called it premature and unofficial. John

Badalich, executive director of the Minnesota Pollution Control Agency, was a quick critic: "There is no evidence," he stated, "that Lake Superior is being polluted by taconite tailings from the Silver Bay plant of Reserve Mining Company."[9] Top officials of the Interior Department joined in the efforts to suppress the Stoddard Report. Pressure from Congressman Blatnik kept Secretary of the Interior Stewart Udall quiet. Just before leaving office on January 20, 1969, however, Udall was paid a visit by U.S. senator Gaylord Nelson, a Democrat from Wisconsin. Nelson told Udall that the newly elected Republican governor of Wisconsin, Warren Knowles, was likely to join the Lake Superior Enforcement Conference on behalf of Wisconsin, thereby triggering a series of hearings on the pollution of Lake Superior by Reserve Mining. Environmentalists at MECCA and the Save Lake Superior Association (SLSA) knew that hearings called by the federal government or one of the governors could result in favorable public interest in stopping the dumping of tailings at Silver Bay. Nelson had long favored the hearings. So Udall called the conference, much to the consternation of John Blatnik and other supporters of Reserve.[10]

Congressman Blatnik reacted to our criticism of Reserve firsthand at the Democratic Convention in Chicago that previous summer. I ran into Blatnik in the men's room during the convention and asked him if he had seen the large picture of the Reserve launder chutes' discharges in the latest issue of *Life* magazine. He immediately accused me of "prejudging" the issue in emotional tones. I heard his criticism of me in more explicit terms after the hearing MECCA held at the Hotel Duluth in March 1969 in preparation for the first Lake Superior Enforcement Conference hearing to be held two months later.

In the three months between the release of the Stoddard Report and this MECCA hearing in Duluth, the press became very interested in the Reserve Mining issue. There was widespread coverage in the *Minneapolis Tribune* by Ron Way, as well as articles in the *Minneapolis Star*, the *Duluth News Tribune*, and the *Duluth Herald*. The Hotel Duluth hearing drew a crowd of approximately 150 people. A number of MECCA board members spoke on various pollution threats to Lake Superior, including the possibility of nuclear power plants being built along the North Shore of the lake. John Pegors, Larry Cohen, and Charles Huver spoke, and my assignment was to address pollution by Reserve. During my remarks I said something about Congressman Blatnik not speaking out against the dumping. It did not take long for whatever criticism I voiced about Blatnik's reluctance to take on Reserve to get back to him.

The week after the hearing I received a call in my office about 4:00 p.m. from Blatnik. He began to harangue me for about forty-five minutes while I took notes on a legal pad. He said I had unfairly criticized him and made him look like an apologist for Reserve Mining. I tried to deny that charge, but it was difficult to get a word in since Blatnik became increasingly belligerent. Years later his successor in the House of Representatives, Jim Oberstar, who had served as Blatnik's chief of staff, told me he had tried to stop Blatnik from calling me and was in the room during the conversation. It was unfortunate. I had known Blatnik since my early involvement in politics and had visited him in Washington while serving in the U.S. Air Force during the fifties. My fellow motor carrier lawyer and partner Val Higgins, who had the office next door, could not help hearing my side of the conversation since my door was open. He came in, wondering what was going on. Finally, Blatnik hung up and I finished making notes on this call from a congressman apparently trying to intimidate me. The notes are with my boxes at the Minnesota History Center in St. Paul.

Time passed quickly between this MECCA hearing and the first session of the Lake Superior Enforcement Conference called by Secretary Udall. During the winter a new environmental group emerged to concentrate on Lake Superior and the Reserve Mining case. Milton Mattson called me in February 1969 to propose a meeting at my home of a few select conservationists to discuss whether there was room for another group. We agreed on a meeting that involved Milton, John Pegors, Chuck Huver, former state representative John Rose, and me. Milton told us of his idea for starting the Save Lake Superior Association. He wanted to be sure there was a need for another organization in the environmental field in

Minnesota. Since today there are approximately eighty-five such organizations in Minnesota and back then probably fewer than ten, it seems hard to believe we debated the need for another. It didn't take long for all of us to agree that SLSA made eminent good sense and Milton was off to begin organizing. Before the May Lake Superior Enforcement Conference he had recruited Arlene Harvell (later Arlene Lehto) to be president. She immediately swung into action and started building a solid SLSA organization with a chapter in the Twin Cities headed by Bruce Blackburn, a Minneapolis lawyer with a Lake Superior summer place on the Brule River in Hovland.

By the time of the May 13, 1969, opening sessions of the enforcement conference, SLSA had recruited dozens of members and worked with other groups such as the Students for Environmental Defense and MECCA to coordinate a strong attack on Reserve with statements, personal testimony, and exhibits.

Shortly prior to this date, I happened to tell law partner Donald Morken of my fear that key information might be withheld from the public at the session. He told me about the federal Freedom of Information Act, which I had not heard about. I looked it up and copied the key provisions in case they were needed.

Another persistent question we raised prior to the conference was whether Governor Harold LeVander would join the conference on behalf of Minnesota, which he had the authority to do under the Federal Water Pollution Control Act. If he had done so, much time would have been saved at the first sessions where it was necessary to prove that the tailings had spread into interstate waters.

LeVander steadfastly refused to join, claiming it was just a political gimmick. As a result, the various environmental groups I have mentioned strongly criticized LeVander and the MPCA for not doing everything possible to stop this pollution by Reserve Mining Company. This did not sit well with the governor's office, and I recall the strong reaction of LeVander's representative at the conference at the first day after we had repeated this criticism. He was a lawyer whom I knew from law school, Larry Koll, and he had some strong words for me because of my criticism of the governor. We did not let that ruin our friendship. LeVander's refusal to join the conference must have been due to opposition from the MPCA chief, John Badalich, who did not wish to relinquish state control of the issue. Both LeVander and Badalich were from South St. Paul.

Although LeVander was on the wrong side of the Reserve Mining issue, he did establish the policy that the state of Minnesota reserved the right to set higher standards for environmental control than the federal government. This policy was followed by his successor, Wendell Anderson. LeVander also deserves credit for appointing Steve Gadler, who became the fiery environmental advocate on the Pollution Control Agency board, even though LeVander's administration later lamented the appointment. LeVander's chief of staff, David Durenberger, recalls that LeVander opposed putting the new Pollution Control Agency in the Health Department. He says the reason was that chief sponsor Senator Gordon Rosenmeier wanted an independent state agency. Rosenmeier had often tangled with the commissioner of health, Dr. Robert Barr.[11]

This first of the six enforcement conferences held over the next two and a half years was full of citizen participation and controversy, with lots of Reserve supporters from Silver Bay. Present were Congressman John Blatnik and staffers from politicians around the lake. More than six hundred people crowded into the historic ballroom of the old Hotel Duluth for the initial meeting.

I well recall crossing the avenue outside the hotel at the same time as Ed Fride, the Duluth lawyer representing Reserve Mining. I pointed to Lake Superior and asked Ed if he ever woke up in the night with his conscience bothering him due to the green water I could see at that time. Ed reacted by accusing me of a low blow and went out of his way to tell me his client had nothing to do with any green water in Lake Superior, if there was any, which he denied seeing. This exchange was a harbinger of things to come at the conference.

Murray Stein from the Water Pollution Control Administration offices in Washington, D.C., and veteran of more than fifty of these conferences, presided together with a panel of three top officials from Minnesota, Michigan, and Wisconsin. John Badalich, together with two citizen board members from the MPCA, Dr. Howard

With Ernie Willenbring at the Minnesota Environmental Control Citizens Association booth at the State Fair in 1969.

Anderson and Bob Tuveson, were the three from Minnesota. Ralph Purdy from Michigan and Tom Frangos from Wisconsin were at the head table. Carl Klein and David Dominick, representing the Department of the Interior and the Water Pollution Control Administration, respectively, rounded out the top-ranking bureaucrats in attendance.

Ed Fride had taken over from his elder partner, William K. Montague, who served as a regent of the University of Minnesota and had handled the hearings in the 1940s for Reserve's predecessor. Fride gave the history of Reserve's operations and called on Ed Schmid, Reserve's public relations chief, and the president of Reserve, Ed Furness, to speak. These three spelled out the company line. The tailings were "mere sand, inert and insoluble in Lake Superior." Furthermore, they argued that the tailings formed a "heavy density current" when they discharged into the lake and therefore flowed right down to the bottom of the "Great Trough" off Silver Bay. Furness also claimed that Reserve was forced to dump the tailings into Lake Superior because it could not build the plant near the Babbitt source of their taconite due to the lack of sufficient water there and insufficient land for tailings disposal.

None of these company contentions held water, so to speak. The company argument about the tailings leaving the two huge chutes and going right down to the bottom because of the so-called heavy density current did not make sense. After a short time the tailings began building a large delta offshore at their property, which meant the tailings went out on top of the delta. When they reached the outer edge they gently spilled into the lake. Dr. Donald Mount, director of the National Water Quality Lab (NWQL) in Duluth, initially called the tailings harmless but soon recanted and testified that the Reserve tailings adversely affected bottom growth in the lake and caused green water in the lake.

Since none of the three state members of this conference officially joined the proceeding, the question of whether the tailings were widespread and crossing over into Wisconsin or Michigan was an issue at this first session. Was there interstate pollution? If so, that would mean this discharge warranted federal jurisdiction. So until the states joined, which they did when the political winds changed direction the next year, this was a major concern.

Before the conference convened, several other environmentalists and I learned that the NWQL, under Dr. Mount, had conducted research on the question of tailings from Reserve crossing into Wisconsin waters. The data showed pollution of the interstate waters. Chicago tough guy Carl Klein, assistant secretary of the Department of the Interior and chair the first day, ordered Dr. Mount to keep these findings from the conference. At this point I decided, with the agreement of MECCA and SLSA, to make a formal demand for the data and study conclusions under the Freedom of Information Act. I prepared a letter request as required and found David Dominick, head of the Water Pollution Control Administration, at a lunch table and handed him our request. Klein then decided that interested parties could view the research results at the NWQL offices near the Lester River on the east side of Duluth. The next day the word spread that the federal officials were not permitting the results to become part of the conference. At that point Congressman Blatnik intervened and instructed Dominick to allow the findings to become public and on the record. The pressure on Blatnik showed as he held an impromptu news conference in the hallway outside the conference room. He had been particularly incensed by an article in the *New York Times* by Gladwin Hill criticizing him for suppression of the Stoddard Report. Perhaps that is why he decided to allow the findings of Dr. Mount's lab to be added to the record of the first enforcement conference.

Intrepid *Minneapolis Tribune* reporter Ron Way recorded how this happened. After pressure had mounted by that afternoon to make the study fully public, Way was alert to something going on when he saw Blatnik, Dominick, and Mount headed for an unused barroom at the Hotel Duluth during a break in the conference. As Tom Bastow relates in his book *This Vast Pollution*, "Way was immediately suspicious, since he knew the rumors that Blatnik wielded his considerable political influence to protect Reserve. Poking around a back hall, Way found a service entrance to the room, eased the door open, and crept on his hands and knees under the bar where the three men sat talking. It was clear, he says, that 'Blatnik was calling the shots—he was dictating terms to these guys.' "[12]

The revelation that Reserve's tailings were discovered in Wisconsin waters was widely reported by the media and was perhaps the most significant development at this first session as it drew to a close after the third day. Shortly afterward, I received a letter addressed to me as chairman of the New Hope DFL club from Senator Walter Mondale on the Vietnam War. Fritz Mondale had handwritten on the bottom, "I saw your Dad in Duluth. Reserve better watch out!"

My father had obviously expressed some strong views about Reserve Mining to the senator. Dad was following the case closely and attended all the conference sessions wearing his "Save Lake Superior" button. He supported what I was doing through the entire thirteen years I fought Reserve, often writing me about the case. Some ten years later Dad and I bumped into Governor Al Quie at the Capitol. Dad had his button on and the governor asked what it was about. Dad told him, "We are working to prevent Lake Superior from becoming another Lake Erie!"

Those of us who prepared hard for the conference and attended all three days were excited that the focus was where it should be—on Reserve Mining at Silver Bay—and by the extensive media coverage, which meant the public was hearing specific evidence and arguments on this pollution. Before the conference there were letters to the editor of newspapers in Minnesota and some newspaper reports, but they had barely made a dent in the public consciousness. I recall making speeches around the Twin Cities, carrying bottles of tailings and receiving good responses from the small groups. After May 1969, public interest was far more intense.

Despite SLSA and MECCA's pleasure with those aspects of the conference, we were not pleased with the foot dragging demonstrated by the Minnesota conferees and especially John Badalich, then MPCA executive director. So we kept up pressure and shortly after the first session in Duluth we enlisted a powerful ally.

In June 1969 the Minnesota State Bar Association held its annual meeting in Minneapolis. One morning Ralph Nader was on the program with Senator Walter Mondale. After their presentations I introduced myself to Nader, told him about our campaign to end the dumping of taconite tailings into Lake Superior and asked him if he would be interested in helping us. He was, and gave me names of his "Nader's Raiders" David Zwick and John Esposito. I followed up with both of them but especially with Dave Zwick, who, along with Marcy Benstock, would author the Nader study group's book *Water Wasteland* in early 1971. I began sending information to Zwick and conferring with him on the phone about Reserve Mining. I also traveled to D.C. to discuss the Reserve case and Dave introduced me to congressional staffers Leon Billings and Tom Jorling, who also proved to be allies. Jorling worked with the Republicans on the Hill and Billings with the Democrats. They were both working on the clean water bill that ended up passing late in 1972.

A year after meeting with Nader and beginning work with Dave Zwick, I got the idea of hiring three law students to delve into the Reserve case and write a book in the spirit of Nader's Raiders. In June 1970, I asked some of my conservation-minded friends what they thought and received encouragement. So I began raising money to fund such a book, which I decided would be titled *Superior Polluter.*

A friend active in the parks and trails movement in Minnesota, and a director of Clear Air Clear Water Unlimited, Thomas Savage, gave me a very nice check to launch the effort. We launched it right afterward and subsequently received support from no fewer than ten environmental groups such as MECCA and SLSA. We also received individual support from David Dalquist, founder and president of the Nordic Ware Company in Minneapolis.

Professor David Bryden suggested students at my alma mater, the University of Minnesota Law School, for me to interview. I selected three who had just finished their second year—Stanley Ulrich, Timothy Berg, and Deborah Hedlund. They began immediate work that summer and by the fall had researched and written a good share of the material that would become *Superior Polluter.* Arlene Lehto, president of SLSA, volunteered to publish the book at her husband's print shop in Duluth. Eileen Bannon did the editing, and the Northern Environmental Council was instrumental in seeing the project through, since I was too busy with the MPCA job I took the next February.

One of the many revelations these three researchers brought to light was the Reserve Mining bias of Dr. John Moyle, aquatic biologist at the Minnesota Department of Conservation, who had testified at the 1947 hearings that "the taconite tailings would have no substantial adverse effects" on Lake Superior. He said there "is no strong current flowing south close to the shore," which later tests showed was wrong. He testified that the "proportion of fine particles that will stay in suspension by the time the water has gotten around that far (to spawning areas south of the plant) would just be so small that there would be practically none to settle out."[13] The students who authored *Superior Polluter* revealed the phony tank experiment discussed previously that was used at the 1947 hearings. They concluded: "To the extent that the decision-makers on the permit application were influenced by the [tank experiment], they were misled."[14] Equally damning was the company's suppression of testimony by University of Minnesota zoology professor Samuel Eddy, hired by Montague to study the impact of tailings deposition on fish and spawning near the plant and then present his findings at the hearings as a witness. Eddy's study found that the tailings would impair the delicate balance of the fish population in a 10- to 15-mile vicinity of the plant. He also placed a dollar figure on damages to the commercial fish catch. When Montague and Oglebay-Norton received Eddy's written findings they did not call him as a witness. Even though he attended the hearings as they requested, they did not introduce his report. Eddy also reported in writing to the company that he was aware of substantial currents in Lake Superior.[15]

At the end of the 1947 permit hearings, Montague represented to Chairman Wilson that no more information was available on currents or the effects of tailings on Lake Superior and urged the hearings be closed. This distorted presentation was just the precursor of the events to follow. Misrepresentation by Reserve would continue for years as the company concealed what the tailings were doing to Lake Superior and how the company was handling the issues both before and during the ensuing litigation.

Until the next session of the enforcement conference, I continued to address various groups and organizing on behalf of MECCA and SLSA. I attended meetings of the Twin Cities chapter of SLSA with members Bruce Blackburn, a Minneapolis lawyer, Alan Bruce, and Hjalmer Storlie, who were present when Arlene Lehto, SLSA president, spoke. Arlene frequently addressed groups on behalf of SLSA and helped keep up the momentum from the first enforcement conference session. She later served several terms in the Minnesota House of Representatives from Duluth.

The second conference meeting, held in October 1969, was an "Executive Session," which meant the public could attend the deliberations but could not make presentations. The conclusion out of this session was that there was "presumptive evidence in the record to indicate that the discharges from the Reserve Mining Company endanger the health or welfare of persons in States other than that in which such discharges originate."[16] The conferees also directed Reserve to prepare an engineering and economic study of maximally reducing its dumping into the lake and submit a report on that study to the conferees within six months of the date when Secretary of the Interior Wally Hickel signed the conference conclusions and recommendations. Hickel did not sign those conclusions until January 26, 1970, almost five months later. He did so despite vigorous political pressure from Armco Steel to water down the conference recommendations, which he refused to do.[17] As Tom Bastow noted in 1969, "Reserve spent approximately $325,000 on lawyers and consultants to defend itself. And Reserve returned approximately $17,500,000 in after-tax profits to Armco and Republic Steel."[18]

One of the top officials of the Interior Department who had publicly attacked the Stoddard Report was Max Edwards, assistant secretary of the department from late 1967 to February 1969. He claimed it contained numerous errors. After leaving this high office with the change of administrations, he was hired by a prominent Washington, D.C., law firm, Collier, Shannon, Rill & Edwards. During the summer of 1969, shortly after being hired, he landed Reserve Mining as a client. On October 22, 1969, the board of directors of MECCA voted unanimously to request an immediate investigation by the Justice Department alleging violation of the conflict-of-interest provisions of the federal criminal code, 18 U.S.C. sec. 207 (a) or (b). These statutes provide that a public official having direct involvement in matters pertaining to a corporation while holding federal public office are prohibited from going to work for that corporation in any capacity for two years following their leaving office. Former attorney general Robert Kennedy wrote the preamble to that section of the criminal code.

After speaking personally with the local U.S. District Attorney Robert Renner about our concerns, on October 30 I wrote to Mr. John Mitchell, attorney general of the United States requesting this investigation leading to grand jury action. On December 16, 1969, I heard back from the Justice Department that our request had been referred to the Criminal Division and that it was under consideration. That was the last we heard of the matter, sad to say. Here was what seemed to us a direct violation of the federal conflict-of-interest law. If that public servant was directly involved in the issue, as Max Edwards clearly was, then he was prohibited from going to work for Reserve Mining for a period of two years.

An Old Fashioned with Robert Traver

One day in the fall of 1970 I received a letter dated October 28, 1970, from John Voelker, "a retired lawyer" from Ishpeming, Michigan. He was writing me because of the publicity about Reserve's daily dumping of sixty-seven thousand tons of taconite tailings in Lake Superior. In looking into who John Voelker was, I discovered that he was in fact a famous author who had retired from the Michigan Supreme Court when his best-selling novel *Anatomy of a Murder* was published under his pen name, Robert Traver. A 1959 movie by that name featured James Stewart, Joseph Welch, Lee Remick, George C. Scott, Duke Ellington, Eve Arden, Kathryn Grant, and Ben Gazzara, with Otto Preminger as director and producer.

For some six months, Voelker and I tossed legal theories back and forth regarding the Refuse Act of 1899 under which the U.S. Army Corps of Engineers purported to issue a permit allowing Reserve Mining to dump "material," not refuse, into Lake Superior. Judge Voelker first wrote on his typewriter but soon reverted to his very legible handwriting. I learned from him later that he always handwrote his books. During these initial months of exchanging legal views on the case, I did not tell him that I knew who he was and he never said anything about *Anatomy* or his many other books. He and I stayed in contact until his death in 1991.

Enjoying a visit with John Voelker (who wrote under the pen name Robert Traver) at his home in Ishpeming, Michigan, in 1978. I'd come to know Voelker while sharing legal theories with him regarding the Reserve Mining case.

In 1978 my family and I were entertained one evening at the home of John and Grace Voelker in Ishpeming. John and I started the evening dinner with his famous Old Fashioneds. His recipe:

Begin with a sugar cube.
Add bitters—not much—on cube.
Cut thin slices of orange and add a cherry and ice cubes.
Add whiskey with a "charitable Christian heart."

During the delicious meal of steamed clams, shrimp, and other seafood, Marilyn asked John how much money he made on the film, a question I would have been afraid to pose. His answer was "enough."

After dinner John showed us his home office, where he wrote his books on yellow legal pads with a green Flair pen. He had signed photographs on the walls from the many stars of the movie and was proud of the wooden desk he had bought years before for five dollars from a local lawyer who was leaving to join a mining company in Cleveland.

In September 1972, before Judge Miles Lord enjoined the MPCA from holding a separate state administrative hearing, I asked Judge Voelker if he would come over to Minnesota and be the administrative judge. He replied that he could not accept and gave me several good reasons. Not long after that he had a fall and ended up in the hospital in Marquette. Grace wrote me about his fall and said John "seems to feel so badly that he turned you down." Shortly thereafter, we were blocked from holding the state hearing that I wanted. And, fortunately, John recovered from the fall and lived another nine years. In the years after he retired at age fifty-five he rarely left his beloved life in the Upper Peninsula of Michigan. He refused to fly, so when he and Joe Welch went fishing in the alpine lakes of northern Italy, they traveled by ocean liner. I feel very privileged to have known him and am glad there is a John D. Voelker Foundation in Marquette that awards scholarships to assist Native American students to pursue law degrees and engages in other worthwhile tributes in his memory.

The First Earth Day

On April 22, 1970, the first Earth Day, a number of gatherings occurred around Minnesota to celebrate the urgent need to restore and protect the environment. I was asked to address the student rally outside the entrance to Coffman Union at the University of Minnesota in Minneapolis, facing the magnificent mall extending to Northrop Auditorium. Over a thousand students and others were present. They heard me stir up action to stop Reserve Mining's pollution of Lake Superior. I urged them to join the growing supporters of on-land disposal required of all other taconite companies in Minnesota. Lake Superior was too precious a treasure to allow the dumping to continue. It was a beautiful early spring day and spirits were high.

Later in the afternoon I drove to River Falls, Wisconsin, to speak at the branch of the University of Wisconsin located there. My friend Charles Carson, professor of geology, had invited me. On the way I stopped for dinner at the Steamboat Inn on the St. Croix River, near the Mississippi River, and while eating read the *Minneapolis Star* newspaper. It had fifteen articles on pollution and the environment. Later at the campus I used the bottle of taconite tailings as a prop during my speech.

I did not mince any words that night in River Falls, saying, "Polluting industrialists are attempting to control our regulatory agencies and suppressing government reports. They are experts in foot dragging and hedging." I referred to the Stoddard Report, which stated that the Reserve tailings causing the green water observed far from the plant were killing the food fish feed upon, causing a public nuisance and violating federal regulations. Reserve Mining had suppressed the federal report for several weeks. By the time the press had finally published it, Reserve had had time to prepare a defense. I explained how the company had dumped two hundred million tons of tailings into Lake Superior through their two "launder chutes" since dumping began in 1956. "Lake Superior is going to hell on two chutes as a result of this dumping," I told the audience of college students. I argued that "the burden of proof for disposal must be changed from 'prove we are polluting' to 'prove you are not polluting.'"[19]

It was very encouraging to see the spontaneous turnouts at these two campus gatherings and the enthusiasm of students about the environment. It was clear to me that the environmental movement was growing. The fifteen separate articles in the April 22, 1970, *Minneapolis Star* covered the many issues of cleaning up the environment that people were talking about in Minnesota. When I went around giving speeches, questions concerning burning dumps, nuclear power plants, dirty smokestacks, and litter were often raised.

Sometime around Earth Day, I was also asked to make a speech at Coffman Union, this time inside. I recall giving my usual talk on the Reserve Mining pollution case, emphasizing how the fine fraction of tailings was going out in the lake in suspension and solution. A member of the audience pressed me on what I knew about those two scientific occurrences. I did my best to explain them from my nonscientific background, but this person seemed somewhat unconvinced. I met him afterward. He introduced himself as Ronald Hays, a mining engineer with a doctorate.

Two and a half years later this same Ron Hays wrote letters to then Lieutenant Governor Rudy Perpich on the Reserve pollution issue and those letters came to my attention. We subsequently hired Hays as a consultant for the Minnesota Pollution Control Agency on the case, which was a good move.

Also on Earth Day, U.S. Senator Walter F. Mondale, a good friend of the founder of Earth Day, U.S. Senator Gaylord Nelson of Wisconsin, spoke in Duluth at the University of Minnesota Duluth (UMD). One of Mondale's aides, Michael Berman, who grew up in Duluth and attended Duluth East High School and UMD, told Mondale that he could not give a speech there without addressing the Reserve Mining issue. Fritz Mondale took Berman's advice and said that Lake Superior was a priceless resource that deserved high protection, and that the state and federal governments should see that the permits issued to Reserve were enforced. We took what Mondale said as tantamount to supporting on-land disposal of the tailings now going directly into Lake Superior. After all, there was no other way to meet the permit condition restricting the tailings to a nine-mile zone outside Silver Bay.

A key result of all the student enthusiasm exhibited on this first Earth Day was that many students became active in organizations such as the Minnesota Environmental Control Citizens Association and the Save Lake Superior Association. Some of them became activists with Students for Environmental Defense and other groups working to stop pollution. I have a picture of the crowd outside Coffman Union that typifies the interest on that first Earth Day. I was proud to have been a part of Minnesota recognizing that prompt environmental action was needed.

Minnesota DFL Politics

After 1968 my political involvement on the local and state level turned into more and more citizen action and organizing. I came across an article in a bar association publication about a new law adopted in Michigan and written by Professor Joseph Sax, the Michigan Environmental Protection Act (MEPA). This was a breakthrough in environmental law that gave individual citizens and groups standing to sue polluters. Once the plaintiff proved pollution, impairment, or destruction of the water, air, or natural resources to a material adverse degree, the burden of proof shifted to the defendant. The defending party then had to show that there was no feasible and prudent alternative. Economic considerations alone could not constitute a defense. In May 1969, I had lunch at a downtown Minneapolis restaurant with state senator Wendell Anderson, whom I knew from the 1968 National Democratic Convention in Chicago and the 1968 Humphrey Minnesota campaign, which Anderson headed. He was then testing the waters for a race the next year for governor of Minnesota and brought along his campaign adviser, David Lebedoff, a Minneapolis lawyer. During lunch, I mentioned the Sax "MEPA" law. Anderson showed immediate interest, saying he would like to introduce it in the Minnesota state legislature before the session ended in a few days.

With Congressman James Oberstar in St. Paul, December 1999.

I was impressed when Anderson's aide Jim Weiler arrived at my law office that very afternoon to pick up the copy I had of Joe Sax's proposed Michigan environmental law. Wendy Anderson promptly introduced it in the last days of the 1969 legislative session. This action showed me Anderson's political interest in environmental issues as well as his quick action as a politician.

Despite my contact with Anderson, I initially supported a law school classmate, Warren Spannaus, for governor. He did well in the early campaigning but decided to leave the gubernatorial race to run for attorney general. That was when I supported Anderson, one of the leading three candidates. The other two were state senator Nick Coleman and Professor David Graven. Others in the race up to the state convention were Hennepin County Attorney George Scott, Bob Short, entrepreneur and former owner of the Minneapolis Lakers basketball team, and Russell Schwandt of the Minnesota Agribusiness Association.

In April 1970 I ran for chairman of the Third DFL Congressional District. I sought the post at the request of the state chairman, Richard Moe, and ran against a fellow from the Minnetonka area who had been campaigning for several months. I prevailed at the Third District convention in May. Shortly thereafter, Wendy Anderson visited me one night at my law office, where I was writing a law brief, and asked for my support. I said yes and became the first congressional district chair to endorse Wendy. He ran a splendid campaign and in June won the endorsement of the DFL state delegates at the state convention in Duluth on the sixth ballot.

After Anderson's endorsement on June 25, 1970, I was approached on the convention floor by state senator Rudy Perpich to support him for lieutenant governor. I had talked to him during his campaign about the Reserve Mining issue. I would go for him the next day.

The next morning my dad and I drove to the Duluth Entertainment and Convention Center on the Duluth waterfront, where the state convention was held. I noticed a number of Tom Byrne for Lieutenant Governor signs around the convention. I thought this was odd, since he had not been campaigning for the job. I was soon visited by an Anderson aide, who told me that "if I knew what was good for me I would support Tom Byrne for lieutenant governor." To me he was not a good choice since he was from St. Paul, where he had served previously as mayor, and Wendy Anderson was from St. Paul. I just looked the aide in the eye as I reached inside my sport coat where I had hidden my blue Perpich button, and pinned it on my outside lapel, thinking as I did, "There goes a Supreme Court appointment." Not that I had ever coveted such an appointment. I certainly had not talked about any appointments with Anderson, but I did think it was a bit strange that only twelve hours after my candidate was endorsed for high office I was crossing him. I was sure Wendy was supporting Byrne by this time, even though Dave Lebedoff denied it.

Interestingly, I later learned from state senator Nick Coleman's son Patrick Coleman that after Anderson beat Nick and Dave Graven for the endorsement, Hubert Humphrey and other DFL leaders summoned Nick Coleman to a boiler room meeting and insisted that Nick should be the candidate for lieutenant governor. Nick said, "No, I supported Rudy Perpich during his campaign and I am not going to renege on that support." With Anderson, Spannaus, and Perpich all winning endorsement, my candidates won and went on to victory in the general election without the primary fighting that goes on now.

The year 1970 was my most successful in politics. In August Wendy Anderson, at my urging, traveled to Duluth to speak to the next session of the Lake Superior Enforcement Conference. By that time, Anderson had embraced on-land disposal for Reserve Mining's taconite tailings. By appearing in person to urge the conferees to adopt that position he focused statewide attention on the issue for the governor's campaign. Only a few days later, his Republican opponent, Doug Head, agreed with Anderson's position for on-land disposal.

Anderson was joined on the campaign trail in 1970 at times by Hubert Humphrey, who had been endorsed in Duluth to run for the U.S. Senate. I recall a Labor Day rally in Anoka where Humphrey chided Anderson for not campaigning hard enough. As the Third

District DFL chair, I followed the various campaigns, but spent most of my time on Anderson's contest and our race for Congress. Humphrey and the DFL leadership had talked longtime WCCO-TV editorial writer George Rice into running and he was endorsed at the Third District DFL convention in May. He was well known for his strong views, but also disliked by many from the Jewish community for his failure to take a strong pro-Israel position. Rice had not been asked to head a WCCO trip to Israel during the preceding year. So when his campaign manager, James Pederson, urged him to make a trip to Israel to shore up his position with Jewish voters in the Third District, Rice said, "If I wasn't good enough for I. J. Fink [owner of a big dry cleaning business in the Third District] last year, I'm not good enough this year," and refused to go. His opponent Bill Frenzel, the Republican candidate, did go and the result was that Rice lost the vote in the heavily Jewish suburb of St. Louis Park by 3–1. Democrats in those days were expected to carry St. Louis Park by at least that margin. As a result, and because Rice would not spend sufficient time on the phone raising money, he lost to Frenzel by one-half of one percent, or 1,250 votes. For years following, I and others referred to Frenzel as "Landslide Bill."

The campaign went well. At one memorable September DFL rally at the St. Paul Hilton Hotel, where some nine hundred Democrats came together to cheer on the statewide candidates, Hubert Humphrey gave the main after-dinner speech and had most of us on the edge of our seats for the first twenty minutes, then he left us wandering after the next twenty minutes. Seeing that he had lost the audience, he attempted to get the crowd back by taking us painstakingly through the Pledge of Allegiance with a speech after every line. That took another twenty or more minutes, and after more than an hour he finally gave up. That was the only one of many speeches I heard Hubert give that bombed.

One other story about Hubert. After he was elected back to the U.S. Senate that fall of 1970, I arranged a meeting between Larry Silverman, top air pollution expert for Ralph Nader, and myself with now Senator Humphrey in his new office. We both sat across from him at his desk for an hour's presentation by Silverman. What I most vividly remember is how taken Humphrey was with Larry's fascinating discourse on air pollution and what to do about it. It was obvious that Humphrey was a keen listener, and I think that ability was as important to his success as his speaking ability. It was as if he grabbed hold of as much knowledge from Silverman as possible in order to store it for future reference. That was a meeting to remember.

Wendy Anderson went on to win the governor's job over Doug Head, and Warren Spannaus won the attorney general's spot. Rudy Perpich was elected lieutenant governor. Thus began eight years of many triumphs for these newly elected officials as well as some of the most significant gains for Minnesota's environment.

The Minnesota Pollution Control Agency

During this time, I was weighing the governor's entreaties that I become the executive director of the MPCA. Besides strong urging by Anderson I received telephone calls from David Lebedoff and DFL state chair Richard Moe trying to convince me to take the post. The decision to leave my law practice was momentous. I had definitely not sought the job and in January had turned down a request by the governor's office to serve on the MPCA citizens board. I was now a junior partner with Mackall Crounse & Moore and things were going well. I enjoyed the motor carrier practice I had been doing for five years after several years of general practice. I was getting plenty of trial practice and brief writing. I liked my partners and the rest of the office.

However, I also knew this was a chance to make a meaningful change in state government and in the environmental arena. I could do a lot more on these issues that I cared about from within government than from the outside. I had accepted the challenge of changing the direction of Minnesota's environmental policies in 1971 largely because of the Reserve Mining Company, but also because I had been involved in the environmental movement since late 1967. As a member of the citizen group MECCA combating pollution, and especially as chair of its Lake Superior Task Force, I learned a lot. My two years in MECCA taught me how to speak in headlines, meaning strong and concise words, as I watched how Larry Cohen handled the battle against Northern States Power Company's new nuclear power plants in Minnesota. He later won the job of Ramsey County commissioner, followed by election as mayor of St. Paul in 1972, and then he was appointed by Governor Rudy Perpich as a district judge in Ramsey County, where he served for years ending up as chief district judge.

I realized then that I could not resist the opportunity to move the Reserve case to a successful conclusion by working from inside government. I was sure I would play a key role toward getting the tailings disposed of on land in a tailings basin, just like all the other taconite companies in the state and elsewhere. I concluded that I could not turn the offer down.

I knew Wendy Anderson was serious about moving ahead on a strong environmental program, not only from visiting with him over the past months but from the fact that his inaugural address on January 6, 1971, contained two full pages (out of thirteen) relating to specific new directions and legislation needed to restore and protect Minnesota's environment. He started out his proposals this way: "Now we know that our first concern must be the preservation of what we have left of the natural resources that sustain our very lives." I also liked his next point: "The people saw the problem first. They provided the leadership for us—the elected officials. Their deep concern remains unserved." Furthermore, Anderson's first official act as governor was to join the Lake Superior Enforcement Conference, which his predecessor, Harold LeVander, had refused to do. Anderson's January 1971 decision led the governors of Wisconsin and Michigan to follow Anderson's action and enabled the conference to drop the previous mandate to prove interstate movement of Reserve's taconite tailings.

So I arranged a leave of absence from my firm and accepted their provision that I could return "all things being equal." I had my law partner and my mentor in the motor carrier department, Don Morken, come over and discuss the whole thing with Governor

Anderson and me in the governor's office. We discussed how I would likely stay a year and a half to two years.

I told Wendy I would do it. So on February 1, 1971, I was present at the governor's reception room where my appointment was announced, effective March 1, along with that of Al Hofstede to head the Metropolitan Council and Larry McCabe as commissioner of aviation. Several reporters interviewed me before starting, including Bill Krueger of KDAL Radio in Duluth. During that interview, Krueger pressed me on two issues in particular—whether on-land disposal of the Reserve taconite tailings would inevitably mean the shutdown of the plant and the loss of jobs at Silver Bay; and whether the active environmentalists in the Twin Cities cared more for fighting pollution in Duluth and northeastern Minnesota than in the Twin Cities. I explained that citizens active on this problem believed that the company could afford to go on land and that it would get a reasonable time to do so. As for the Twin Citians' concern for pollution in the metropolitan area, I cited their opposition to pollution from Northern States Power Company's power plants around the metropolitan area. Krueger's viewpoint was typical of what I heard from others in the Duluth area, even including a close relative of mine who lived in Duluth.

On March 1, my dad accompanied me to my first day in office, since I was to take over my predecessor's state car and Dad would drive my car back home—he was visiting from his home where I grew up in Hunter's Park, Duluth. We drove to the Health Department building adjacent to the University of Minnesota buildings on the Minneapolis campus, and as we drove, I recall asking him about his experience with personnel issues when he served as postmaster in Duluth for thirty years. He told me about several tough decisions where a letter carrier or clerk had to be fired and told me it was important to be fair but firm. My father was an exceptional person, all the way back to his early education in Duluth and in California. He played rugby in high school and football at Pomona College. He served in the army as an ambulance driver in World War I and then worked for several years after the war in New York in the export-import business before returning to Duluth. He told me that morning in the car about having to fire a carrier who had named his son Glen, after him. He came home that day telling Mother and Mary Alice, my sister, "How do I fire somebody who named his son after me?" That was tough, but he did it. He was much admired for his work as postmaster, and as a superb storyteller and keeper of the family heritage. He always had plenty of time for his family, and I was very fortunate to have him around during my MPCA days and until 1991 when he died at the age of ninety-seven.

I was entering this new career with some trepidation, of course. The MPCA covered environmental responsibilities across the board, and I knew I would be under scrutiny because I was determined to make changes in the months ahead. I knew controversy would follow, but I also knew that my degree in public administration and my three years of citizen activism in addition to my legal experience would help in the new challenge of public life.

In taking over responsibility for air, water, solid waste, noise, and nuclear programs, I was also inheriting some eighty state employees. I was quite familiar with the staff and board from meetings in connection with the Reserve Mining case. To one such meeting I took the March 1970 issue of the *Twin Citian* magazine in which I had written the lead article, "The Art of Pollution," about the Reserve case. The cover of the magazine featured a large picture of one of the two chutes dumping taconite tailings in Lake Superior. I had arranged for the photograph from an inside source at the plant, and it powerfully illustrated Reserve Mining's practice. I showed the picture to Ed Fride before the MPCA board meeting began and he immediately objected, claiming the image misrepresented the actual discharge because it looked like the tailings were going directly into the lake. I told Ed he was right—but that where the tailings were going "used to be Lake Superior" and was now the delta created by the earlier dumping.

The night before I began the job, we had relatives at our home when I received a phone call during dinner telling me that a large

THE NEW

Twin Citian

MAGAZINE

**RESERVE MINING IS KILLING LAKE SUPERIOR
BUT THE LIFE SENTENCE WILL BE YOURS**

MARCH 1970

PRICE 75 CENTS

A photograph we arranged to have taken (rather surreptitiously) that
showed Reserve Mining dumping taconite tailings into Lake Superior at
Silver Bay, Minnesota.

spill of jet aircraft fuel was taking place at the Minneapolis-St. Paul Airport. I attempted to reach Lawrence Hall, chair of the Metropolitan Airports Commission (MAC), to no avail. The governor's office gave me the name of the vice chair of the commission—St. Paul mayor Charles McCarty. I called his home about 9:30 that night. His wife told me that her husband was out patrolling somewhere in St. Paul and gave me his phone number. I reached him as he was moving around the city in his "Mayoral Supercar." After I briefed him on the pollution emanating from the airport he said, "Don't you worry about a thing, I will go right out there." With this reassurance I went to bed. About 1:00 a.m. the phone by my bed rang and the mayor said, "Is that you, Merritt?" "Yes, Mr. Mayor." McCarty said, "Were you sleeping?" I replied that I had been. He said, "One thing you need to learn right away—these public jobs are day-and-night propositions. But don't worry. I've taken care of everything." He signed off, saying we would talk in the morning.

Around noon on my first day in office, I convened a meeting regarding the spill, which was in fact 240,000 gallons of jet aircraft fuel into the Minnesota River adjacent to the airport. The Minneapolis-St. Paul International Airport flushed the fuel to a storm sewer, which caused an oil slick up to twenty miles long on the Minnesota and Mississippi Rivers. We summoned all the interested parties to the meeting to discuss the cleanup, which had necessitated using 3M absorbent pads all the way down the Minnesota River and into the Mississippi River. These white pads, floating for miles, absorbed much of the fuel but also demonstrated the need in the future for capturing such a spill before it even reaches the river. MAC changed its procedures after this spill, allowing no more flushing of fuel down the drain to the river.

Mayor McCarty arrived late to the meeting and as he sat down next to me, I whispered to him, "Did you get MAC to pay for the cleanup?" He responded in a loud voice, "Hell yes, they have lots of money out there—all they have to do is open the desk drawer and take it out!" The cleanup cost totaled nearly half a million dollars. This episode on my first day in office was dubbed my "baptism by fire" by a reporter.

That afternoon I began drafting a letter for the governor to send to the general in charge of the U.S. Army Corps of Engineers asking to revoke Reserve Mining's permit, with two years to comply by building an onshore tailings basin. Wendy signed it and sent it to the corps by telegram. After Anderson joined the Lake Superior Enforcement Conference, EPA administrator William Ruckelshaus took his own action to expand the scope of the conference to include the "navigable waters of Lake Superior and its tributary basin within the State of Minnesota."

Five days later, I attended a meeting of the technical committee appointed by the enforcement conference to discuss Reserve Mining's proposal for deep-water discharge. Reserve hoped to hide its dumping through underwater pipes so the public wouldn't see what was happening. I was there representing the MPCA, and Reserve's lawyer Ed Fride attended as an observer. I informed the group that the position of the state of Minnesota, as decided by the new governor, was that the tailings from Reserve must go on land as soon as possible. That helped to kill the Reserve plan of further dumping into Lake Superior, infuriating Fride. He soon thereafter attacked this effort of mine as "prejudging" the case, similar to the attacks I had earlier received from Congressman John Blatnik.

Wendell Anderson's first official act as governor was to join Minnesota as a full party in the interstate enforcement conference proceedings on Lake Superior. Patrick Lucey, governor of Wisconsin, joined soon thereafter. This was an important development for those of us involved in the federal enforcement conference still under way on Lake Superior, as it meant it was no longer necessary to prove the interstate movement of the taconite tailings from Silver Bay. Anderson decided to attend the next session of the conference and invited me to fly to Duluth with him. At the session on January 14, 1971, he again urged the conferees to require Reserve Mining to build a tailings pond onshore and thereby cease dumping into Lake Superior. Anderson specifically opposed the "deep pipe plan" proposed by Reserve, which would have continued the dumping of tailings in Lake Superior with the addition of an organic flocculant to the new underwater discharge. Professor Robert Bartlett in his book *The Reserve Mining Controversy* said:

> Both governors got political mileage out of attending the enforcement conference. It was an opportunity for two Democrats to show that they were doing something where Republicans appeared to have been fiddling around. After rumors about the deep pipe plan had been confirmed, but before this session of the conference had been convened, Grant Merritt and Charles Stoddard discussed the matter with Anderson and Lucey, emphasizing that the plan probably would be accepted unless a stand was taken against it. And in his statement to the conference, Anderson did declare that Minnesota would insist on onshore disposal. Both governors called for onshore disposal at a news conference the same morning.[20]

This joint stand by the two governors, plus the continued full court press by the citizen activists, undoubtedly blocked the conference from adopting Reserve Mining's deep pipe plan. The conferees established a technical committee to study on-land disposal and Reserve's underwater disposal plan and report back in sixty days.

Later that month, I appeared before the Senate Civil Administration Committee for my confirmation hearing. Before the committee session began, the Republican chairman, Senator Wayne Popham, called me aside for a brief introduction and then said to me, "Just remember, Grant, we Methodists must stick together." The hearing went quite smoothly despite pointed questions on Reserve Mining by Republican senator George Pillsbury and one or two others. I was recommended favorably for confirmation and then confirmed by the Senate.

In those days there was bipartisanship at the legislature. Republicans controlled both the House and Senate, yet the legislative proposals of the Democratic governor Anderson received decent treatment for the most part. I think this was partly because Wendy Anderson had served in both the House and Senate and had established strong and favorable relationships with many key Republican legislators as well as DFL members.

Early on in the new job I called a meeting of the staff and urged them to join in becoming more aggressive in cleaning up the environment. I said I had no objection if they wanted to become active in one of the environmental nonprofit organizations as long as it did not interfere with their jobs. I explained the new state policy for on-land disposal of the Reserve Mining tailings at Silver Bay and a bit about how I saw this policy would be carried out. I also told them of my activity in the Minnesota Environmental Control Citizens Association and Save Lake Superior Association and said the staff should become advocates for the environment, with the board acting as the policy maker. We staff members would advocate on water, air, and solid waste as well as the newer environmental issues. There were no problems from this new staff policy. I think they got the message that I was serious about the MPCA pursuing a strong advocacy role on behalf of clean water and air.

By hiring strong pollution fighters to work along with the staff already there, it was my plan to reverse the "regulatory capture" that enabled, for example, the MPCA to forward complaints about Reserve Mining dumping to Reserve Mining Company officials to answer the complaints. In addition to bolstering the staff advocacy role, we hired Jim Dunlop as the agency public information director who opened up the MPCA to full transparency. This led to a much more informed citizenry. We took steps such as creating a new division of special services to look for solutions to problems that focused on better choices to prevent the problems rather than just seeking temporary solutions after the problems arose. The idea of this new division was Chuck Carson's, my tough deputy director.

Although I was in charge of the MPCA staff, and the agency advocate for the environment, I was, of course, responsible also to the governor. Wendy had selected the Second Congressional District DFL chairman, Tom Kelm, as his chief of staff. I had spent time with Tom at the state convention in Duluth the previous summer and at Hubert Humphrey's summer home in Waverly, Minnesota.

Tom Kelm's reputation was as a tough, no-nonsense politician who had followed his father, Elmer Kelm, to the top ranks of the DFL Party. Tom had a photograph on his office wall that showed Elmer Kelm and President Harry Truman smiling at each other. In early 1944, President Roosevelt summoned Elmer Kelm to the White House, where he explained he was worried about carrying Minnesota that fall because of the existence of two parties competing for Democratic voters—the Farmer-Labor Association and the Democratic Party. Roosevelt asked Elmer to go back home and attempt to merge the two parties in time for the presidential election that fall. Kelm followed Roosevelt's suggestion and with the help of chief assistant, Hubert Humphrey, succeeded in merging the two parties, with the result that Roosevelt carried the state.[21]

Wendy Anderson could not have chosen better than Tom Kelm. My first work session with Tom was in his office, which was adjacent to the governor's office. The meeting was to discuss the Reserve Mining case. Tom knew that there was opposition at the Department of Natural Resources to the governor's announced policy of on-land disposal of the Reserve tailings. Commissioner Bob Herbst, my counterpoint at the DNR, two lawyers representing the DNR, Phil Olfeldt and Paul Farici, and Bill Brice from the DNR's Minerals Division were also present. The DNR four argued against on-land disposal, claiming a tailings pond would interfere with possible new state parks behind Silver Bay.

In a meeting of department heads that occurred shortly after they were sworn in but before I took office in March, Tom Kelm had given a short speech in which he pointedly stressed that they should "remember who brought them to the dance!"[22]

So at the meeting in Tom's office he informed the DNR staff that the policy of this administration was to stop the dumping and that the tailings were to go to a tailings pond on land. There was to be no further opposition by DNR—that was it. No undercutting, nor further talk of problems with on-land disposal. Naturally, I was extremely pleased with the way Tom "laid down the law," directing the DNR representatives to get on board with the new policy. Shortly thereafter Tom sent me a brief memo suggesting I hire a young woman from his office, Jackie Burke. I happened to know that Ms. Burke had attended an early environmental conference out east and that she would be an asset to the MPCA, so I told Tom to send her right over.

Tom and I were not always in perfect harmony, of course. He once told a newspaper reporter that he spent 25 percent of his time dealing with issues involving me. In 1974 I arranged a reorganization of staff at the MPCA, which by statute required approval by the commissioner of administration, Dick Brubaker. He granted that request. I later appointed a new director of water quality, Bob Hamilton—who had a master's degree in toxicology and before coming to the agency had worked at 3M. Immediately after I announced his appointment, both the Minnesota Society of Professional Engineers and the Minnesota Association of Commerce and Industry threatened to hold a news conference blasting me and the governor as antiengineering. They complained to Kelm, who then called Brubaker and ordered him to rescind his approval of my appointment of the nonengineer Hamilton. I said to Dick Brubaker, "You can't do that. He's already begun working as director of water quality!" Dick said he had no choice in light of Tom Kelm's order. That gave me thoughts of resigning. I either had to accept the decision or resign, I thought. I decided to abide by the order and stay on, and my deputy John Olin and I had to search for an engineer to replace Hamilton.[23]

Years later I lunched with Dick Brubaker, and he remembered my attempted reorganization. We reminisced about Tom Kelm and he reminded me of Kelm's admonition about never forgetting who brought you to the dance. He also told me another Kelm story. Tom had a red sport coat and a green one. Whenever he wanted to alert members of the legislature where the governor stood on an issue, he would enter the back of the chambers wearing red for a no vote and green for yes, thereby signaling how to vote on a particular issue.[24]

After leaving the MPCA job, I also enjoyed some very good conversations with Tom Kelm when I served as consultant to the governor on Reserve Mining matters. He told me about a meeting at the governor's residence involving him, Wendy and William Verity, CEO of Armco Steel, and others from Reserve. After social pleasantries, they discussed where the tailings basin should be located. Verity and company said Reserve wanted at a future date to announce they were going to the Lax Lake area inland from Silver Bay and did not want to be blasted on that site like they had been by Governors Anderson, Lucey of Wisconsin, and William Milliken of Michigan at a previous Midwest Governors Conference on the Palisades Creek plan. Kelm told me that no deals were made at the meeting and that the company was told it would get a fair hearing on its proposal. He also said that the group discussed pollution control financing.

During the first weeks in office, I helped craft the governor's Special Environmental Message to the legislature. I worked with Duane Scribner of the governor's office, and also James Pederson, who chaired George Rice's congressional campaign the previous year. As I recall, Scribner was Wendy's chief speechwriter and a full-time member of his staff. The message was a thirty-three-page document that he delivered in person to a joint session of the legislature. It was titled *Restoring and Preserving Minnesota's Environment*.

Stressing that "our water, land, and air have been damaged and continue to be damaged," he urged the legislature to amend the Minnesota constitution to provide for an environmental bill of rights and substantially increase funding for the MPCA. He outlined a twelve-point proposal for new programs needing action by the legislature. The first point of his proposal was for environmental rights legislation that would give private citizens the right to sue polluters with the provision that the burden of proof would shift to the defendant once a prima facie case was established. This legislation was patterned after the Michigan law drafted by Joseph Sax. As mentioned previously, Anderson had introduced a bill to establish this MERA, Minnesota Environmental Rights Act, at the end of the preceding biennial session in 1969.

The new governor had stressed in his inaugural message the need for stronger enforcement of pollution laws. He said informed concern for the environment should become part of every governmental decision. He urged passage of an environmental policy act that would "require consideration of the environmental impact of every state, regional or local decision affecting the physical surroundings." Next he recommended establishment of a $180 million fund for construction of municipal sewage treatment facilities, which together with the federal share of the cost, would reduce the municipality share from 70 percent to a maximum of 25 percent. He also urged extension of MPCA authority to regulate noise pollution. He called for a moratorium on construction of new nuclear power plants in Minnesota—"of indefinite duration, lasting until the Pollution Control Agency certifies, under appropriate legislative standards, that risks have been eliminated and new development can safely begin."

This was the most ambitious environmental program ever proposed by a Minnesota governor, and much of it was passed in the 1971 legislative session and succeeding sessions. These twelve proposals were in addition to Anderson's earlier recommendation for a major staff increase for the PCA, support for the creation of Voyageurs National Park, and an end to Reserve's dumping.

The municipal sewage program passed with the support of local governments in 1971. The state share was set at 15 percent, the federal at 75 percent, leaving 10 percent for municipalities.[25] Wendy's environmental proposals showed just how tough he was as governor. He proved that time and again.

Wendy Anderson's service as governor will long be known for major accomplishments in the environment and education. He was a strong leader and widely admired. He was able to push innovative programs through both the Republican legislature of 1971–72 and the Democratic controlled legislatures of 1973 and 1975. In the 1971 session, the Minnesota Environmental Rights Act was passed with bipartisan support within weeks compared to Michigan where it took months to pass in its legislature.

On April 12, 1971, the Ralph Nader–sponsored book *Water Wasteland*, authored by David Zwick and Marcy Benstock, was released. It received front-page coverage in the Sunday *Minneapolis Tribune*. The book had a full chapter on the Reserve case titled "Better Late Than Never: The Lake Superior Story." The *Tribune* story highlighted a confidential memorandum by Reserve's public relations man Ed Schmid to Ed Furness, the president of Reserve. The memo proved to be a bombshell. It showed how the company influenced a trip by Secretary of the Interior Stewart Udall to inspect Reserve from an airplane. Reserve arranged for motel rooms in Duluth for some members of the Udall party and started the day with a "Bloody Mary" breakfast at the Kitchi Gammi Club in Duluth. Ed Schmid wrote that he would arrange for Mike Lubratovich, assistant director of the National Water Quality Laboratory in Duluth, to be on the plane with Udall because "he's one of our strongest and best-informed supporters and could serve as a Reserve 'spokesman' with Udall as well as being 'our eyes and ears, too.' " Schmid also told Furness in this memo that Reserve would plant grass seed on the tailings delta where the big discharge chutes were located so that "much of that delta can be green, attractive and obviously stable."

These Sunday revelations created a great deal of comment and reaction by the public, as can be imagined. And, of course, Congressman Blatnik was not happy. The headline, on the separate front-page story containing the entire confidential memo by Schmid, was "Reserve Sought to Better Its Image."

Taconite Tailings

Exactly one year after the Earth Day events of 1970, I assumed my new role as Minnesota conferee. On April 22, 1971, I attended the next session of the Lake Superior Enforcement Conference in Duluth. After the publicity from the *Water Wasteland* revelations, the mood at the enforcement conference in Duluth was more favorable than it had been earlier regarding on-land disposal of tailings at Silver Bay and the new policy in Minnesota endorsed this solution. I joined MPCA board members Dr. Howard Anderson and Robert Tuveson, and returning to Duluth as conference chair was David Dominick, acting commissioner of the EPA water quality office. Except for me the cast of characters was pretty much the same as at earlier sessions.

Speaking for the Northern Environmental Council, an environmental umbrella group including the Save Lake Superior Association, Charles Stoddard urged the conferees to find an alternative disposal method. After retiring from federal service, Stoddard had stayed in Duluth and organized this group. He said:

> As long as the initiative is in Reserve's hands, there will be continued political wire-pulling, manipulated studies by kept scientists, drummed up litigation, court challenges, and misleading public relations propaganda. The funds spent by Reserve for these purposes not only insure continuance of the extraordinary high profits derived from polluting the lake, but an infinite number of conferences. . . . Weak political compromises and legal maneuvering are no longer acceptable. . . . Lake Superior is in many ways an historical test of our nation's Will to clean up environmental pollution.[26]

My favorite memory of this conference session centered on a motion I made on behalf of the three Minnesota conferees that on-land disposal must replace dumping in the lake. First, of course, I had to get the support of Bob Tuveson and Dr. Howard Anderson, both of whom had previously supported my predecessor, John Badalich, in the earlier proceedings. Both were appointees of the Republican Harold LeVander, who had gone along with Badalich. But in this instance, they agreed with me on the motion.

Before the conference convened I met privately with the new conference chair, David Dominick. Upon entering his room at the Hotel Duluth, I noticed he had a copy of *Water Wasteland* with him. This encouraged me to discuss a motion I had in mind that would instruct the administrator of the EPA to notify Reserve that it was violating federal water quality standards and had 180 days to come up with an acceptable plan. The administrator could then ask the Justice Department to sue Reserve if it did not come up with such a plan. During this time the EPA would hire an independent consulting firm to advise them on whether Reserve's plan was acceptable.

During the session, my motion was adopted by the conferees. I then made the further motion that the conference go on record in favor of on-land disposal for Reserve's tailings. After some debate the three states and the federal government passed that motion unanimously. This was a big step forward, because the federal government now was in agreement with our new Minnesota policy of on-land disposal. Dominick then went on to urge his boss, Bill Ruckelshaus, to move under the Federal Water Pollution Control Act, which he did.

When the official summary of the April 1971 session of the conference came out shortly afterward, it did not contain the second motion unanimously endorsing on land disposal. I immediately wrote to Ruckelshaus, asking that the minutes be amended to reflect this action by the conferees, which led to a meeting in Minneapolis with Governor Anderson, Ruckelshaus, and me in the backseat of Anderson's limo, with Wendy's press secretary, Ted Smebakken, in the front seat. Smebakken wrote after the meeting on October 14, 1971, that Ruckelshaus "agreed to include the Federal government as a party to endorsing on-land disposal in a corrected summary and conclusions statement." Bill Ruckelshaus did as he said he would.

The EPA 180-day notice to Reserve expired on October 25, 1971. And the Weston Report, costing the EPA $100,000, was a "virtual nullity."[27] Heavy lobbying ensued at this point by the owners of Reserve, Armco, and Republic Steel Companies. Their "backstairs political manipulation and influence-peddling" included meetings with top EPA and White House staffers. Despite this political pressure, on January 20, 1972, the Lake Superior Enforcement Conference action enabled Bill Ruckelshaus to send a public letter on January 20, 1972, to the Justice Department requesting a lawsuit against Reserve.

However, before Ruckelshaus could send this letter to the Justice Department, he had to get White House approval. He met with John Ehrlichman in the White House and was given the go ahead.[28] Bill Ruckelshaus deserves plenty of credit for maneuvering this approval through the Nixon White House. According to attorney Byron Starns, Ruckelshaus made a deal with the Nixon White House that he could start the federal lawsuit against Reserve—but not against Reserve's owners Armco or Republic. According to Tom Bastow in *This Vast Pollution,* however, it is difficult to confirm this story.

On February 17, 1972, the Justice Department filed suit against Reserve in federal court in Minneapolis. The suit called for an injunction to require Reserve to abate its pollution, not for on-land disposal. Whether there was a deal preventing Ruckelshaus from alleging on-land disposal is also unknown. Judge Miles Lord of the District of Minnesota was designated by the court to hear the case.

The states of Wisconsin and Michigan joined the Justice Department as coplaintiffs, as did several environmental groups including the Save Lake Superior Association. Minnesota did not join for several months as I was concerned that we preserve the state's right to pursue legal action in state courts if the federal action did not prevail. Specifically, while I was not troubled by how Judge Lord would handle the case, I was mightily concerned about the Eighth Circuit Court of Appeals in St. Louis, partly because of the way that court had handled my grandfather's case some eighty years earlier. Judge Lord finally resolved this after I argued my position against the famous Robert Sheran representing Reserve. Bob Sheran was shortly to be appointed to the Minnesota Supreme Court by Governor Anderson, and it was a pleasure to match points with him again as I had done early in my career when he was first on the Supreme Court. Soon after oral argument, Judge Lord called me telling he was going to "join us and enjoin us" from further contesting Reserve in state court. Thus we joined the plaintiffs. Our lawyers were first Jonathan Morgan and then Byron Starns, who tried the case for Minnesota and the MPCA.

In preparation for trial we decided that we needed an expert economist to analyze the financial statements of Reserve Mining Company and its two parents, Armco and Republic Steel. Our lawyer, Jon Morgan, suggested to me University of Minnesota professor Glen Berryman, head of the accounting program at the university, who had been a witness for Attorney General Head during the 1970 state trial against Reserve in Two Harbors.

So we called Dr. Berryman over to the MPCA offices in the Health Department to discuss hiring him. After meeting and discussing what we wanted, Jon Morgan and I decided we would hire him to consult for the MPCA and later testify before Judge Lord. Jon prepared the retainer agreement and sent it to Dr. Berryman.

Several weeks later he showed up at my office. Shaking his head, he said he was sorry he could not work for us. He told me that his boss, the dean of the department, said "it would not be in the best interest of the U of Minn. for him to do this project." I said, "What! You mean we can't hire one member of the faculty to work in the public interest when there are a half dozen over there working for Reserve Mining?" I told him to go back and get that in writing. He went back and conveyed my message and the dean backed down, enabling us to hire him, which we did and he did an excellent job. My notes from this episode also show that John Hills, chief counsel for the federal government in the trial before Judge Lord, told me that "Berryman had been directed by William Shepherd, vice president of the university, *not* to testify in the Reserve case."

Since then I have had lunch with Dr. Berryman to confirm my recollection of this incident and he well remembered it. I also had a chance to tell this story to President Bob Bruininks of the university, at the first showing of the four-hour documentary *Minnesota: A History of the Land,* which has a fifteen-minute segment on the Reserve case. Bruininks's comment on the dean's rejection of our hiring Berryman was "that should not have happened."

One of the University of Minnesota professors who supported Reserve happened to be a member of the MPCA board. He was the renowned Dr. John Borchert of the Geography Department faculty. His term on the board expired after my first meeting with it in March 1971. He spoke to me at that time and earlier in public in favor of Reserve Mining's position on using Lake Superior to deposit its tailings. He wrote a letter to the *Duluth Herald* on January 13, 1970, when he was on the MPCA board, arguing that it was "ridiculous, unfair and short-sighted to take picks on one of our foremost employers in Northeastern Minnesota (Reserve Mining Co.)." He went on to argue that taconite tailings were inert rock, which, of course, was Reserve's propaganda line. Borchert's premise was that to push for on-land disposal would "force another good citizen out of our state."

Establishing Environmental Policies

In those first months, I was faced with a policy-making board of neither my nor Governor Anderson's choosing. This slowed the kind of progress I had in mind. We did move along much of the MPCA's work, however. Anderson had appointed two new members to the board—Dr. Dale Olsen from the University of Minnesota Duluth, and Harold Field, an attorney from Minneapolis. Together with holdover Steve Gadler, that meant a 6–3 vote against our positions on some of the large industrial polluters such as Reserve Mining and Northern States Power. It took a year for Anderson to achieve a majority on the board with the appointment in January 1972 of Marion Watson and Joe Grinnell. I found, however, that if I made a good enough case for action, the board generally supported me even in that first year.

The MPCA board was unique in the nation as part of a state environmental regulatory body. My role was to implement the legislative mandates as well as the policies adopted by our citizen board. I sat with the board at its meetings, but was not a voting member or the chair. As a result of the innovative structure, developed by Senator Gordon Rosenmeier from Little Falls, the public became directly involved in our work, which was covered extensively by both the print and electronic media.

Rosenmeier was a powerful state senator in Minnesota who commanded respect for his creative approach to legislating and had a powerful presence that often intimidated fellow senators. Wendell Anderson later told me he had felt intimidated by the senator when he was himself in the state senate.

According to a Rosenmeier chief aide, Blair Klein, Rosenmeier regarded state bureaucrats as in general lacking the fundamental vision to make policy. This showed in his dealings with the state Health Department and its commissioner Robert Barr. Rosenmeier often went after Dr. Barr at legislative hearings with his exceedingly sharp skills at cross-examination.

This distrust of state employees also became evident in Rosenmeier's creation of the MPCA. The law that he sponsored in the 1967 session provided that the governor appoint the first executive director who would then decide which, if any, of the employees at the predecessor water pollution control agency, housed in the Department of Health, would be transferred to the new agency. After Rosenmeier was defeated in the 1970 election, he appeared in my first year in office before the MPCA citizens board on behalf of a client, Hennepin Paper Company. Seated with the board, I observed how he was immaculately dressed and delivered one of the best presentations by a lawyer I had ever heard. There was no question that his request on behalf of Hennepin Paper would prevail. After the meeting, I introduced myself and invited him up to my office. I asked him about how he created the agency I now headed and during the visit he went over to my bookshelf and selected the volume of statutes from 1967. He read the language about transfer of employees. He said he was still perturbed that Governor LeVander did not appoint my predecessor until November 1967 instead of immediately after the agency began in July. By the time the first director arrived in November, all the pollution control employees from the health department had become members of the MPCA.[29]

After my MPCA days were over, I again had several visits with Gordon Rosenmeier at gatherings of the Minnesota Historical Society. At one such encounter I mentioned to him that I appreciated how as director of the MPCA I was in the role of advocate for policies and positions before the citizens board. He commented something to the effect that he wasn't sure he had someone like me in mind as the advocate, which gave us both a good laugh.

The open-door policy that I initiated with the help of the agency's director of public information, James Dunlop, helped us get the news out around the state. We used to inform reporters of what was happening, whether it was good or bad. This helped our credibility and was instrumental in saving the agency when a legislative initiative attempted to bury the PCA in the DNR. With Jim's help we had an excellent relationship with the key reporters and invited them to sit in our top staff meetings if they had some interest in the policy being discussed. During my years at the agency, I got acquainted with Garrick Utley of NBC, who covered one of the hearings in Duluth on Reserve. It was an honor to meet him. I was also interviewed in my office after the Reserve decision by a local reporter for WCCO-TV and that interview was played on the *CBS Evening News* with Walter Cronkite that night. At Isle Royale the following summer, Bob Green, a fellow Tobin Harbor resident, insisted on calling me "Cronkite Merritt."

No other state agency had this type of media policy. It worked well with the citizen policy-making board. Reporters would arrive almost weekly to dig for stories. Even though this occasionally caused me grief because of stories we would have preferred not make the public airways, it kept the agency in the news, which built our reputation around the state.

As an agency that expanded from some eighty-plus employees to two hundred when I left in June 1975, we began to augment the preponderance of engineers with biologists, geologists, and other specialists to create a multidisciplinary cadre of experts. This would pay off in the years ahead. For example, I hired Dr. Charles Carson to set up a new division named Special Services which soon included expertise in nuclear power plants, "ban the can" or deposits on beverage containers, reduction in plastics, recycling, and source reduction of solid waste. Jackie Burke turned out a massive report on recycling, Karen Wendt a similar work on regulating plastics, and Ken Dzugan prepared us for an effort to pass a nuclear moratorium in the legislature. Russ Doty represented the agency at the legislature and worked on legislative proposals. Today, the agency has over eight hundred employees.

Two weeks after I started my new job I was faced with my second baptism—this time truly by fire—enforcing the agency's ban on burning in front yards. The city of Minneapolis was stalling on compliance and the agency board authorized me to begin a lawsuit against Minneapolis if the city council failed to approve an agreement to comply.

I met with a council subcommittee at City Hall on March 26. This was the first time the media covered what I was doing, and after some heated discussion, the council went along with enforcing our regulation. In return, we gave Minneapolis an extension until July 5 for compliance. Mayor Charlie Stenvig had previously said he favored our regulation. Mayor Charlie McCarty of St. Paul was already enforcing the ban. So the ban went into effect without the necessity of a lawsuit, and there were few complaints.

At the same agency meeting authorizing the lawsuit to enforce the burning ban, the board debated whether to support the citizen suit bill, MERA, which the governor and I favored. The board favored the citizen suit concept unanimously but voted 5–3 to require the citizen plaintiff to show injury from the pollution when attempting to change PCA standards. Dale Fetherling, the *Minneapolis Tribune* reporter covering the environment at that time, reported that I opposed the agency position at the board meeting because the injury requirement was "diametrically opposed to the whole concept of the citizens' right to sue polluters."

The MERA legislation faced stiff opposition at the legislature that spring and if it hadn't been for the persistent support of a small group of Minneapolis lawyers, it never would have passed. The lawyers were Dick Flint, John Broeker, and Charles Dayton from the Gray Plant Moody law firm and Will Hartfeldt formerly of the attorney general's office but in 1971 in private practice. They had begun meeting on Saturday mornings in the fall of 1970 for two to three hours working off the Michigan bill drafted by Professor Sax. They arranged to have Rolf Nelson introduce the bill in the House; Edward Gearty, William Kirchner, and Wayne Popham authored the bill in the Senate. The bill followed the usual circuitous path through both the House and Senate, where it encountered opposition from the Minnesota Association of Commerce and Industry, farm groups, and other industry representatives. It was supported by the Sierra Club North Star Chapter, the Izaak Walton League, the League of Women Voters, and the Citizens League. Dick Flint testified in support before both House and Senate committees. My notes indicate I attended the House Judiciary Subcommittee for the debate on H.F. 284 at which lawyers Dayton, Flint, Broeker, and Hartfeldt all testified in strong support.

After several hearings and amendments the MERA bill passed and was signed by Governor Anderson on June 7, 1971 (Minnesota Environmental Rights Act, MN Stat. 116B). The bill had several prominent features, among them: (1) citizens and Minnesota government could seek injunctive relief, both temporary and permanent, to protect the state's natural resources from pollution, impairment, or destruction; (2) once a showing is made of such damage to the environment to a "material adverse degree," the burden of proof shifts to the defendant to prove that there was "no feasible and prudent alternative" and that "economic considerations alone shall not constitute a defense." I recall being in the Senate Gallery when the Senate debated the bill and watched Jack Davies attempt to amend the bill to delete the language regarding economic considerations. His amendment was defeated by a close vote.

So MERA passed, thanks to that small group of lawyers from Minneapolis who worked hard to build support for the bill and successfully negotiated with the legislators involved. It wasn't long before MERA was tested by Bill Bryson, a farmer who objected to a road proposed by Freeborn County through a wetland. Will Harfteldt and a law classmate of mine, Larry Downing, represented the Sierra Club, which intervened on behalf of Bill Bryson. The case was *Freeborn County by Tuveson v. Bryson* (210 N. W. 2d 290; August 31, 1973). After a rehearing on remand Bryson prevailed thereby blocking the county from building the road (309 Minn. 178, 243 N.W. 2d 316; June 18, 1976). Ironically, the Tuveson mentioned was the same Tuveson I referred to earlier as a member of the agency board when I began in early 1971. When his term expired a year later he held a news conference blasting the work I was doing at the agency. He was the county attorney who lost the Bryson case. Some of my staff had fun with his news conference, putting together a handout with Tuveson's picture and some of his choice parting words.

In early 1971 the governor designated me as the Minnesota representative to a group of state and federal officials in Washington, D.C., drafting the executive agreement between the United States and Canada on Great Lakes pollution. This was an educational experience because it enabled me to see how the Nixon White House was influencing the work of the group. Notes from the administration would be handed to the group dictating what was wanted and what would be rejected.

In December 1971 the *Wall Street Journal* published a short article titled "Agency Official Asks Federal Aid to Strengthen Proposed Pact on Great Lakes by U.S., Canada." I made this request in a letter to Russell Train and Bill Ruckelshaus of the Council on Environmental Quality and the EPA, respectively. The article stated: "Grant Merritt, Minnesota adviser on the team negotiating the agreement, said it should specify that secondary waste treatment and phosphorus removal be required of all sources discharging into the Great Lakes and their tributaries."

Unfortunately, this proposal did not end up in the final product, no doubt because Canada did not require secondary treatment of all dischargers to the Great Lakes, preferring instead to require secondary treatment only where it thought it was necessary. That is still the Canadian policy. In 1971, for example, the city of Thunder Bay used only primary treatment, resulting in essentially raw sewage going into Lake Superior. In the summer of 1972, I arranged a sampling trip for several MPCA biologists, my deputy, Chuck Carson, and myself. We left from Grand Marais and sampled water quality at several locations in Thunder Bay. One of them was in front of a large grain elevator near the entrance to the McIntyre River, where we found the oxygen level was zero with methane bubbling to the surface. That data was published in a report that is now baseline data for comparison in any future sampling at the many places where we sampled, including Isle Royale National Park.

This drafting work went on throughout 1971 and culminated in the Great Lakes Water Quality Agreement signed in Toronto, on April 15, 1972, by President Richard Nixon and Prime Minister Pierre Trudeau. It was not a full-fledged treaty because Nixon did not want to submit it to the Senate for ratification. It contained lofty goals as well as specific means to clean up the Great Lakes and was the start of bilateral work by the neighboring countries that has continued to the present day.

I was invited to attend the celebration of this new effort on the Great Lakes on the eighth floor of the State Department in Washington, D.C. It was the highest diplomatic event I ever attended. I had brief meetings with Secretary of State William Rogers, conveying greetings from Governor Anderson, and Mitchell Sharp, Canada's minister of external affairs, as the foreign secretary's job was then known. At the luncheon I sat across from Henry Diamond, New York's environmental chief. Other top directors from the eight Great Lakes states also attended.

On December 8, 1971, Chuck Carson and I attended the hearing on the Clean Water Act in Washington, D.C. This legislation had previously passed the Senate and was dubbed the Muskie Bill. We first heard David Zwick, coauthor of the book *Water Wasteland,* who delivered a virtuoso performance before the House Public Works Committee in favor of strong cleanup provisions. Zwick had studied water pollution the previous two years along with colleagues under the auspices of Ralph Nader, and was among the Nader staffers known as "Nader's Raiders."

The next day I was again in the same hearing room for testimony by my boss, Governor Wendy Anderson. I sat right behind him and Governor Nelson Rockefeller of New York. I remember seeing Rockefeller's elevator shoes. The hearing room was full for the testimony but one prominent member was absent—New York congresswoman Bella Abzug. Many in the room knew of the tense relations between Ms. Abzug and Governor Rockefeller and eagerly awaited her arrival. Just before Rockefeller was to testify Abzug arrived wearing one of her ever-present hats. The governor testified that the United States could not afford the proposed legislation, that it would cost the country three trillion dollars. Ms. Abzug, a skilled trial attorney, cross-examined Rockefeller, asking, "Just how did you arrive at that figure, Governor?" Rockefeller said, "Very simply, Madame Congresswoman—I figured out what it would cost to clean up an estuary in New York and then extrapolated from there to the country!" A few more questions and the governor was reel-ing. In desperation he said, "I thought my figure was pretty good, but it isn't nearly as good as your beautiful figure!" Those are the words I heard. The official transcript of the hearing states it dif-ferently: "Governor Rockefeller: 'The distinguished Representative from New York has questioned my figures. My concern is that in challenging my figures, she has none to substitute, except a very beautiful figure of her own.' Mrs. Abzug said 'Thank you. [Laugh-ter.] That is one demerit for you, Governor.' "[30]

Whichever way it was said, the room of some two hundred peo-ple erupted in laughter. The chair, Congressman Bob Jones of Ala-bama, filling in for the sick John Blatnik of Minnesota, let the uproar go on for several minutes before using the gavel. Ms. Abzug glared at Rockefeller during the uproar and when it quieted down told Rockefeller, "We aren't going to continue on that level, Governor." Peter Vanderpoel, editorial writer for the *Minneapolis Tribune,* was there and wrote an editorial published the next day titled, "Pan-demonium in the House." He criticized Bob Jones for letting the crowd reaction go on so long. It was indeed a day to remember.

Throughout my four-plus years on the job I traveled extensively around the state speaking to groups of citizens on all aspects of the environmental movement. I also attended meetings outside Minne-sota. On June 8, 1971, I delivered a speech to the Rural Cooperative Power Association on the subject of a nuclear power plant proposed by United Power Association (now Great River Energy) to be lo-cated at Aitkin. The speech was prepared at my direction by Ken Dzugan, our specialist at the MPCA on nuclear energy. At the out-set I pointed out that the early nuclear power plants constructed at Elk River, and the Pathfinder plant in South Dakota, "were less than successful."

I mentioned that a bill imposing an indefinite moratorium on new nuclear plants had been considered in the 1971 session of the Minnesota legislature and that it had my support, the support of Governor Wendell Anderson, and many groups and individuals from around the state. The bill did not pass that year, but I said, "I am certain, however, that the concern of Minnesotans did not die with this bill" and that another attempt to pass such a moratorium would be made in the 1973 session.

The speech outlined the problems of licensing reactors, the dangers of large amounts of cooling water necessary at the reactors, and the Price-Anderson federal law limiting liability for nuclear power plant owners. I pointed out that the dual and conflicting role of the Atomic Energy Commission, promoting and at the same time charged with regulating nuclear power plants, was frustrating to state regulatory bodies such as the MPCA.

Finally, during 1971–72 we continued to challenge federal preemption of state standards on both air and water discharges of radioactivity from the plants in Minnesota. This challenge was begun under the previous administration and we carried it to the Eighth Circuit Court of Appeals in St. Louis and ultimately to the U.S. Supreme Court. The Eighth Circuit upheld the decision by U.S. District Court Judge Edward Devitt favoring NSP and preemption by a 2–1 vote and the Supreme Court affirmed. That meant that until Congress reversed the preemption, both air and water discharges were regulated exclusively by the AEC.

As an interesting sidelight, in April 1971, Robert Engels, the president of Northern States Power Company, which owned the nuclear reactors at both Prairie Island and Monticello, promised the MPCA that even if the company won this legal battle of preemption, NSP would meet the state standards, which were stricter than those of the AEC. Unfortunately, David McElroy, Engels's successor, asked the MPCA to release NSP from this commitment to abide by the state standards. I recommended to our board that we hold a public hearing, which we did in July 1972 in a large hearing room in the State Office Building. Dale Fethering, the environmental reporter for the *Minneapolis Tribune*, wrote, "About 250 persons attended the meeting which mirrored the diversity of opinion about the health effects of nuclear-plant emissions." At the end of the hearing, Robert Hudnut, president of the Greater Metropolitan Federation, said in a ringing voice to NSP, accompanied by thunderous applause, "You said you would do it, now do it!" At the next MPCA meeting, the board voted to hold NSP to its pledge to meet the state standards. NSP promptly reneged on its promise. It was most unfortunate that Bob Engels had retired before this decision by his successor not to honor the promise to meet our state standards. I admired Engels for this and other decisions he made and said so publicly.[31]

When Wendell Anderson later represented Minnesota in the U.S. Senate, he successfully advocated legislation reversing the federal preemption for airborne emissions from nuclear power plants. Unfortunately, Minnesota and other states have not pursued this opportunity to set higher standards than those of the federal government.

I remain convinced that the efforts of the MPCA, as well as those of citizen activists such as those in MECCA, played a significant role in the decision by United Power Cooperative to drop its plan to build the nuclear plant near Aitkin, Minnesota. To substantiate my conviction, a former MPCA staff member, Russ Doty, tells me that the United Power Cooperative lobbyist discussed with the company my adamant opposition to building a new nuclear plant—that I had pledged I would "fight you all the way"—and that rather than continue, the company chose to build a fossil fuel plant in North Dakota and "wheel" that power to Minnesota by a large power line, which later in the 1970s was itself the subject of considerable controversy because of the high-voltage power lines.

An even more powerful reason why Minnesota had a de facto moratorium on building any new nuclear power reactors, until the legislature enacted one in 1994, is the serious accident that occurred at NSP's Monticello reactor in the fall of 1971. On November 19, 1971, the torus—a donut-shaped concrete structure beneath the reactor building—broke, causing some fifty thousand gallons of radioactive water to flow into the Mississippi River. I summoned key agency folks to what I called a "war room" and kept in touch with Dr. Warren Lawson, commissioner of the Minnesota Health Department, who decided that the threat to public health from this radioactivity headed to the Twin Cities was grave. He ordered the city of Minneapolis to shut the intake to the Minneapolis drinking water treatment plant that uses Mississippi River water. That catapulted the Monticello accident into national news, sending a shock wave around the country. The incident ended up on the *CBS Evening News*. I remember keeping copious notes as we were dealing with the crisis that I dictated into a memorandum to the MPCA board immediately afterward. It contained quotes from telephone calls I had with NSP's Rollie Comstock. That memo somehow got into the hands of Comstock and he let me know he did not appreciate being quoted. After this incident we negotiated an alarm system with NSP so that we would be alerted to any future discharges of radioactivity.

As part of the MPCA proposals to the Minnesota legislature in 1973, we again raised the nuclear plant moratorium issue first endorsed by the governor in his environmental message two years earlier. The board wrestled with the idea. After much heated public discussion, in a dramatic finale following a tied 4–4 vote, Chairman Homer Luick broke the tie in favor of the moratorium. We helped in drafting legislation and Representative Willard Munger passed the bill in the House Environment Committee. Senator Nick Coleman, by that time the Democratic-Farmer-Labor majority leader in the Senate, agreed to author the bill. He could not, however, get the Senate Environment and Natural Resource Committee to pass the bill out of committee. That and the fact that Governor Anderson reversed himself and did not support the bill, killed the moratorium. Of course, the skillful lobbying behind the scenes by Brainerd Clarkson, chief lobbyist for NSP, and others on behalf of NSP, also helped the company succeed in killing the administration's support for our moratorium bill.

Before the start of the Reserve litigation, other problems needed my attention. In early June 1972, members of the Operating Engineers Local 49, representing the employees at the state's largest sewage treatment plant, Pig's Eye, located downstream from St. Paul on the Mississippi River, called in sick, resulting in a shutdown. This caused some 250 million gallons of raw sewage to flow into the Mississippi River without secondary treatment. Because I had served on the MECCA board for over two years with Larry

Cohen, I immediately called him in his capacity as mayor of St. Paul to discuss the crisis. We agreed that the PCA and the city of St. Paul would sue the Metropolitan Sewer Board for an injunction to require these public workers to end their "sick-out," which we accomplished in short order. As I recall, I met with the union head, Frank Zaragoza, on a Sunday at the Pig's Eye plant and discussed a settlement. I took my then four-year-old daughter, Carolyn, with me to the meeting. Negotiations worked and we were able to end the "sick-out" within two or three days.

During the summer of 1972 I attended the first of many meetings of the Great Lakes Water Quality Board (GLWQB), established by the new U.S.-Canada Great Lakes Water Quality Agreement, as the Minnesota member. The first meeting was held in Windsor, Ontario. The International Joint Commission (IJC) members were there to get us started. The board was made up of representatives of the eight states bordering the lakes, the provinces of Ontario and Quebec, and the federal governments of Canada and the United States. We reported to the IJC. After getting acquainted we began our business. The major action of our board was to convince the IJC that it should hold a series of hearings around the Great Lakes to gather citizen testimony on how to carry out the agreement's objectives. Our recommendation was accepted by the IJC. In addition, several of us successfully argued that the Upper Lakes Reference Group, also established by the IJC, should report to our board rather than directly to the IJC. I recall that the IJC took this idea under advisement during lunch, and when the commissioners came back the U.S. chairman, Christian Herter Jr., announced their decision, agreeing with our recommendation. Then he added: they would "ride your ass" to see that we do the job.

I had help from staff in doing the work on this agreement. One who helped throughout my three years on the GLWQB was John Pegors, whom I had appointed to head the new district office in Duluth. By law, his appointment had to go to the agency, meaning the board. Representatives from the Minnesota Society of Professional Engineers and an engineering professor at the University of Minnesota were there to object to John's appointment because he was a plumber, not an engineer. This opposition was rather quickly quashed by the board. In particular, I remember board member Marion Watson reacting swiftly and with a deft dagger when Walter Johnson from the university said, "Some of my best friends are plumbers, however," claiming they are not qualified. These outside "experts" seemed to believe, as did engineers inside the agency, that these new district offices should all be staffed with engineers. John was confirmed and became one of the ablest and hardest-working members of my team. I appointed him to the Upper Great Lakes Reference Group and his work there was most successful.

Later I had to appear before the Minnesota State Professional Engineers Association to defend myself against charges that I was not appointing enough engineers at the MPCA. I recall there were some sixty separate engineering groups present. I was at the podium for well over an hour answering questions. Finally, one member got up and obliquely defended me by stating that he believed that not all engineers make good administrators. I thought I would get a break and sat down. It wasn't forty-five seconds before the presiding official gaveled the questioner down and summoned me back to the podium to answer more questions. My defense to all these questions was that yes, we needed engineers but we also needed other disciplines in this new environmental battle, and that I believed a multidisciplinary approach was needed.

One of my problems with sanitary engineers in those early days of the 1970s was their too-frequent dependence on dilution as the solution to pollution. In addition, I concluded we needed more than just secondary treatment sewage plants for the larger cities. In other words, we should push for tertiary treatment, which meant no more than one part per million phosphorous in the plant discharges. The Metropolitan Sewer Board in the Twin Cities did begin to require tertiary treatment for its newer sewage treatment plants.

During the next three years I attended many meetings in Toronto and Windsor, Ottawa, and Washington, D.C., to carry out the Great Lakes Water Quality Agreement between the two countries. Our recommendations would go to the IJC. If the IJC agreed, it would send the recommendation "to the governments." One initiative of mine was to stop the discharge of ballast water used by saltwater ships entering the St. Lawrence Seaway. I was concerned that this ballast water would spread invasive species throughout the Great Lakes. I recall that it was Ira Whitman, Walt Lyon, and I, representing our respective states of Ohio, Pennsylvania, and Minnesota, who pressed hard for pumping out ballast water from vessels entering the seaway.

Unfortunately, we could not gain the consensus of the board. The shipping industry strongly opposed the proposal and influenced the two federal governments, the provinces, and the other five Great Lakes states. The failure of our effort was most unfortunate. Had we succeeded in passing our resolution, perhaps the introduction of the destructive zebra mussels in the Great Lakes in 1986 could have been prevented. Scientists have discovered that the zebra mussel and other invasive species have been introduced since that time by the discharge of ballast water from ships originating in Europe and elsewhere. Just as with the Reserve Mining Company, we seem destined to deal with serious pollution problems after the fact with expensive cleanup measures and perhaps litigation, when prevention could have completely avoided the problem.

Also in the summer of 1972, after a brief vacation with my family at Isle Royale National Park, I returned to my office to see a full-page newspaper ad by Northern States Power pinned to my office wall by my public information director, Jim Dunlop. The ad had run in both the *Minneapolis Tribune* and *St. Paul Pioneer Press* and blasted me for the MPCA's refusal to grant NSP's request to be relieved from its commitment to meet our state permit standards at its nuclear plants. The newspaper ads contained major misrepresentations of the facts and caused me to respond forcefully in my executive director's report to the next agency board meeting. My strong reactions were reported on the front page of the *Minneapolis Tribune* by Dean Rebuffoni, and in the *Pioneer Press*. My comments were also top of the TV news that night. The reaction of NSP was swift and personal.

I'm in Trouble with My Old Law Firm

Within weeks of this incident I visited my old law office, Mackall Crounse & Moore, in downtown Minneapolis and told my colleague Don Morken (who had accompanied me to visit with Governor Anderson when I was considering taking the PCA job) that I was ready to carry out my intention to leave the PCA and return to the firm. I had planned to stay a year and a half and had a written leave of absence agreement that I could return "all things being equal."

Don said there were problems and told me how within days after I had lambasted NSP, partner Clay Moore had attended a luncheon meeting of the Corner Club, which met in those days at the Minneapolis Club. Fellow member Charles Horn, president of Federal Cartridge in Anoka and a member of the Minneapolis Housing Authority, had asked Clay, "Isn't that Grant Merritt a former partner of yours?" Yes, Clay said. Well, Horn said, "I will see that he never practices law again in Minneapolis." What set off Horn, who was a client of the firm, was my attack on the misrepresentations by NSP in the nuclear matter. Clay Moore was shaken by the threat as can well be imagined. Both the housing authority and NSP were clients of the firm.

I had once attended a luncheon of this Corner Club, a small and exclusive group, with Clay's father, Perry Moore, who was a law classmate of Horn's at the University of Minnesota Law School many years earlier. At that luncheon Horn related a story to us about how he had been in Washington, D.C., at a function where then Attorney General Robert Kennedy was present. Horn told us how he turned to another attendee at the event and asked in a loud voice—which he often did because of poor hearing—is "that son of a bitch over there Bobby Kennedy?"

Mr. Horn was not only outspoken but also cut a powerful path in those days, sporting an impressive handlebar mustache turned up and curled at each end. His clout was felt around town. Naturally, when Clay Moore reported back the threat to his partners, I was in trouble trying to get back to the firm where I had worked for eight and a half years and where I had become a full partner two years before leaving. The partners told me that I had stepped on too many toes and that I was not to be welcomed back.

That rejection hurt plenty because I had always liked the firm, even though I was the only Democrat there. It caused me a lot of regret over the next several months. I always assumed that David McElroy, president of NSP, was behind Horn's vehement outburst, but could never prove it. Both McElroy and Horn have been dead for many years, so I never will know why Charlie Horn decided to unleash his diatribe against me. In retrospect, I probably should have refrained from my strong comments about the NSP newspaper ads, but my motive was to let the public know how NSP acted. I came close to calling them fraudulent, which they likely were. Anyway, a state public official does not often make such statements about powerful corporate interests. NSP frequently had staff members in the audiences at speeches I made around the state and had lined up dozens of law firms to protect its flanks.

I told Wendy Anderson about what happened, and he tried to smooth things over by asking Edward Murphy, president of Murphy Motor Freight Company, one of my old firm's clients that I had represented, to intercede with Mackall Crounse & Moore on my behalf. That changed nothing, but I appreciated their help.

Staying at the MPCA for another three years was to my benefit in the long run. I was able to see the Reserve case through the trial and much of the aftermath, remaining as a special adviser to the governor on the Reserve case until he left office to become a U.S. senator in early 1977. This longer experience in the environmental field proved helpful to my future law practice. Serving a full three years on the Great Lakes Water Quality Board was also a great experience.

In 1980 President Jimmy Carter deregulated interstate trucking with the Motor Carrier Act. Congress preempted state trucking regulation in late 1994. I lost a considerable portion of my client base as a result, and it was fortunate that I had the environmental background to focus on that specialty. I spent the next years handling environmental issues around the state mixed with some lobbying at the Minnesota capitol.

During the fall months of 1972, I was full of depression over losing my chance to return to my old law firm. It became difficult to work, but I bore down and kept going all the while thinking back on my decision to give up my old practice and firm partnership. I started to fight the depression by writing an article for the first issue of *Minnesota Ecology*, "Agency Aids Citizen Fight." I referenced a comment made by a prominent Democrat, Texas congressman James Wright, later Speaker of the House, during consideration of the Clean Water Act of 1971: he said, "I'm interested in people—to hell with the fish!" My comment then, just as applicable today, was that "lack of understanding of the delicate ties between man and his environment thus continues at high levels." I made the point that strong environmental and citizen groups "can help keep government on track and, equally important, provide support for governmental actions which tread on powerful toes. Those interests which feel threatened by pollution abatement and prevention will invariably apply pressure at the top levels of government. To offset and counteract this continual lobbying effort, citizen groups must apply equal pressure in the public interest if environmental restoration and protection are to be realized." That statement obviously reflects my reaction to the pressure on my old firm from Charlie Horn.

During the fall of 1972, I also felt the aftereffects of a speech in which I called for a moratorium on copper nickel mining on the Iron Range until a comprehensive environmental review of this potential activity could be done. I called for the environmental review to be conducted over the rest of the 1970s. Unfortunately, the *Minneapolis Tribune* misquoted me as calling for a moratorium until the end of the century. Still quite new at handling the media, I decided to let the misrepresentation go unanswered, thinking it would pass away soon enough. How wrong I was.

Before long I learned that Mayor Jack Grahek of Ely, and several others from the region, paid a visit to the governor calling for my resignation. I was also summoned to a meeting with Senator Walter (Fritz) Mondale, who said he heard about my speech when he got off a plane up north. This was during his campaign for reelection in the fall of 1972. He criticized my remarks, but I don't remember his exact words. By this time I was getting used to being chewed out by politicians.

On the other hand, we received good help on congressional issues from both Congressman Don Fraser and Mondale. For example, the MPCA prepared a statement in support of the bill allowing states to "completely prohibit the discharge of sanitary wastes from boats." Russell Doty of my staff prepared a draft that Fraser used with some modification to support this proposed legislation. We also rounded up Minnesota environmental groups in support of this amendment, which passed and was incorporated into the Clean Water Law. Ultimately in 1972 the Muskie Clean Water bill was passed over the veto of President Nixon. Both Mondale and Fraser were personally supportive of the bill.

Reserve Mining and Asbestos

The end of 1972 saw the emergence of the public health issue in the Reserve Mining case. It first arose at the December 7, 1972, hearing of the International Joint Commission in Duluth. This was the second IJC hearing held on Lake Superior after the Great Lakes Water Quality Agreement went into effect. The first was held at Thunder Bay, Ontario, on December 5. John Pegors, our Duluth regional director, and I drove up there to attend. IJC member Louis Robichaud, former premier of New Brunswick, chaired the public meeting. I did not testify at this hearing, but Ed Fride, Reserve's chief counsel, gave a long speech about how Reserve was the pioneer in taconite production, which allowed the industry to develop. He went on to say there was no material effect from the green water and "nobody knows what causes it." A number of Canadian citizen activists testified. Some of them were critical of Reserve's pollution of Lake Superior.

During the day I discussed with Fride the confidential negotiations, which our lawyer Jonathan Morgan had recently initiated with my approval. Fride correctly predicted that he "didn't hold out much hope of success." His prediction proved correct as the discussions came to a quick end. I recall that this trip was a great help in lifting my spirits after three months of depression and ended this down period in my life. I still had recurring hopes that somehow I would get back to the law firm. On our way back to Duluth, we stopped at John's cabin on the shores of Lake Superior in Hovland, and called MPCA board member Marion Watson to tell her that I would be returning to the agency for the hearing on APC-17, our proposed regulation on airborne asbestos emissions. That meant I would not be able to attend the IJC hearing in Duluth on December 7. John Pegors and Lovell Ritchie from the home office would cover this hearing.

Just before the IJC hearing in Duluth, I received a letter from Vice President Olga Madar of the United Auto Workers. Olga Madar had long served Walter Reuther at the UAW, continuing after his death as vice president and director of the Department of Conservation for the UAW. She had been informed of the Reserve case and this hearing by Verna Mize, our strong citizen advocate in Washington, D.C. Madar scheduled a meeting for the night before the hearing at the Radisson Hotel in Duluth. She sent her letter to "Friends of Lake Superior," encouraging a big turnout for the IJC hearing and inviting them to dinner and what she termed a "pre-hearing conference" the night before. The purpose of this evening dinner meeting was to "discuss testimony for the hearing and future strategy in efforts on behalf of Lake Superior."

Two special friends of Lake Superior attended Madar's gathering—Arlene Lehto, president of Save Lake Superior Association, and Joe Mengel, professor of geology at the University of Wisconsin–Superior. Mengel had heard about the meeting but thought it involved the red clay runoff from the south shore of the lake, a specialty of his. When there was a break in the meeting he left, but Arlene followed him to the hallway. Mengel told her that he had recently read an article in *Science* magazine by R. R. Merliss, MD, about how talc used by the Japanese in polishing rice was causing stomach cancer in Japanese citizens. Talc is often contaminated with amosite asbestos. The fibers in the picture accompanying the article looked to Mengel strikingly similar to fibers he had seen in iron formations, such as those being extracted at Reserve's Babbitt mine and crushed for its Silver Bay plant on Lake Superior.

Lehto followed up on this information later that night with her son. They read about asbestos. The next day she testified at the IJC hearing about the Reserve tailings dumping and included a carefully worded paragraph raising the possibility of Reserve's tailings causing cancer. John Pegors communicated this testimony back to me, and I summoned my deputy, Charles Carson, our chief counsel, Jonathan Morgan, and Dr. Ed Pryzina to my office to discuss this news.

Dr. Carson soon jumped up and ran out of the office down the hall to look at a geology book. When he came back, he slammed the door to my office and exclaimed, "Eureka, we got them!" That certainly got our attention in that memorable meeting in my Health Department office. The first decision was that Deputy Director Carson would investigate and find a neutral scientist to test the theory that the tailings contained fibers that were potentially cancer causing. We all agreed that we would keep the investigation confidential so as not to inflame the public with fears of cancer until we had evidence of such a serious threat. Carson immediately arranged to hire a geologist, Dr. Stephen Burrell at the University of Wisconsin–River Falls, to analyze fibers that we would collect from the Babbitt mine, the launder chutes at Silver Bay and from the pelletizer emissions into the air around the plant. We arranged for John Pegors and other staff to collect samples. They were delivered to Steve Burrell, who began the study. He prepared thin slides and had Dr. Stout at the University of Minnesota in Minneapolis analyze them using an electron microscope.

During the time Burrell and Stout were doing their work, in April 1973, Attorney General Spannaus transferred our attorney Jon Morgan to the capitol to become solicitor general and appointed Byron Starns to be our chief lawyer. Starns also assumed the job of chief counsel for the MPCA and the state of Minnesota in the Reserve Mining case. Byron had a good background having graduated from the University of Chicago Law School before joining

At my office at the Minnesota Health Department in the spring of 1973. Photograph by John Croft, *Minneapolis Tribune.*

the attorney general's staff. He did litigation while there and was in charge of the opinion section of the office. Shortly after he arrived at the MPCA offices, Deputy Carson shared with him our investigation on whether there were asbestos fibers in the tailings at Silver Bay. Byron went right to work on this public health issue as well as on the overall preparation for trial, which was coming up in the summer of 1973. He proved to be an excellent lawyer for both the MPCA and Minnesota in the forthcoming nine-month trial before Judge Lord.

In the meantime, the EPA lab in Duluth responded mildly to Lehto's testimony at the IJC hearing in Duluth. Lab employee Dr. Philip Cook returned to his offices and briefly mentioned to Dr. Gary Glass the possibility of Reserve's tailings causing cancer. Both of them dismissed it as either "irresponsible" or "unfounded." They did not pursue the issue until May 21, 1973, when Glass told Cook about a dream he had during the night that he should not drink the

Duluth water. Cook immediately found the Merliss article in *Science* magazine to which Joe Mengel had referred at the Madar meeting the previous December. Both Cook and Glass conferred with John Hills, the federal government chief counsel, who instructed them to discuss the issue with experts. They did.

At approximately this same time, Starns notified Hills that we had been alerted to the asbestos issue in December and had retained Dr. Steve Burrell for the study, which he and Dr. Stout were conducting. From then on, Byron, John Hills, and Hills's colleague Tom Bastow worked closely together as a team representing the federal government, the state of Minnesota, and the MPCA.

Following several meetings involving top administrators at the EPA headquarters in Washington, John Hills flew to New York City and spent an afternoon with Dr. Irving Selikoff at the Mount Sinai School of Medicine. This led to the preparation of a witness statement by Selikoff. That was then hand-delivered to Judge Lord in the presence of Robert Sheran, representing Reserve. Judge Lord held several closed court meetings to decide what to do, culminating in a meeting with all lawyers present. I was there because Judge Lord sent a note by phone to the PCA, delivered to me at an agency board meeting. The note summoned me to an immediate meeting in Judge Lord's courtroom. Chuck Carson realized the importance of this and suggested going along with me.

When we arrived we knew something critical was involved, seeing all the lawyers seated with solemn faces. A federal marshal was posted at the door to keep out the public. Seated at the counsel table with the lawyers on our side of the case, I was asked by Judge Lord if I knew what was going on. I gave that some thought before answering and said no, but I could perhaps guess. Lord asked me to explain and I told him how we had been informed by John Pegors about the possibility that the Reserve tailings could cause cancer and that we had hired a geologist in December 1972 to analyze the Babbitt mine, the tailings, and the airborne emissions for asbestos. I said the consultant's report was nearly finished and that I expected it shortly. It arrived immediately thereafter.[32]

Soon thereafter Don Boxmeyer, environmental writer for the *St. Paul Dispatch,* learned about the issue and broke the news the afternoon of June 15, 1973, in a boldface front-page headline: "ASBESTOS-TYPE FIBER FOUND IN DULUTH WATER."

On behalf of the MPCA, I issued a press release that summarized the Burrell Report. The asbestiform-type amphiboles were found in the taconite mined at Babbitt, throughout the crushing processes, in the "exhaust stacks of the pelletizer plant," and in the discharges from the two large launder chutes into Lake Superior. "These amphibole minerals are in every way identical to the amphibole minerals amosite and actinolite which elsewhere constitute commercial deposits which are mined for the production of asbestos," I said.

The Minnesota Experimental City

Along with the drama over the Reserve asbestos news, four other issues commanded our attention at the MPCA. President Nixon impounded funds appropriated by Congress for sewage treatment; we rejected the proposed location of the Grand Portage Hilton Hotel; the MPCA made a serious effort to pass legislation to "ban the can," as we called the proposed beverage deposit law; and we held a hearing directed by the legislature to determine the environmental impact of a proposed development known as the Minnesota Experimental City.

At one of our staff meetings, after hearing about Nixon's defiant impoundment of sewage treatment funds that Congress had appropriated for treatment plants in Minnesota, I asked our chief lawyer whether we could sue President Nixon for this action. Jonathan Morgan researched it and told me we had a good cause of action against the EPA for carrying out the president's order without first conducting an environmental impact statement pursuant to the National Environmental Policy Act of 1970. On the basis of that advice the agency authorized the lawsuit. It was filed in U.S. District Court in Minneapolis on March 7, 1973. The MPCA won a verdict there for $121 million. The Eighth Circuit Court of Appeals overturned that verdict. The funds were restored by the U.S. Supreme Court, however, giving Minnesota back a total of $171 million—-$121 million for Nixon's 1973 impoundment and $50 million for another impoundment in January 1974.[33]

Later in 1974, the very first article of impeachment filed against Nixon was based on his illegal impoundment of these sewage treatment funds appropriated by Congress. Dave Zwick says Reagan did the same but nobody sued him!

Early in 1973 the Grand Portage Band of Lake Superior Chippewa pushed a proposed Hilton hotel that would be built far out on Raspberry Point at the southwest end of the large bay at Grand Portage. Our staff rejected this location as posing a water pollution threat because the site was so close to Lake Superior. We also raised questions about a potential threat to surrounding timberlands. The band had submitted an environmental impact statement, but we found it deficient. The federal Economic Development Administration was ready to provide three million dollars in loans and grants for the hotel, but it said quick approval was needed due to the Nixon administration's plan to phase out the EDA within three months.

Within two weeks of the objections we raised at the MPCA board meeting on March 26, 1973, Governor Anderson stepped into the controversy on the side of the Grand Portage Band. He directed his economic development commissioner, James Heltzer, to go to Washington to meet with Congressman Blatnik and the acting assistant head of the EDA. Chuck Carson was quoted in the *Minneapolis Star* on this development as saying, "I don't know if helping Conrad Hilton is the way to help the Indians." Needless to say, that comment did not go over well with the governor's office.

The controversy soon passed when we met with the leaders of the Grand Portage Band and agreed on a compromise. The hotel location was moved back, away from Raspberry Point, and construction began shortly later. The hotel is now the Grand Portage Lodge and is run by the band. It has an adjoining casino whose earnings have allowed band members to improve their standard of living. Because I have left from the Grand Portage dock on the other side of the bay to go to Isle Royale many years since 1952, I recall how Grand Portage tribal members there lived in tar paper houses in the fifties, sixties, and into the midseventies. Many of the homes in those days were dependent on outside wells. Now the houses look like other houses found across America. The outcome benefited the environment and the economy of the area.

In the 1973 legislative session, we supported legislators in their efforts to pass a "Ban the Can" measure, imposing a deposit on beverage containers. Such a law would provide a real incentive to recycle beverage containers, since there would be a payment of, say, ten cents a can, as Michigan provides, for turning in empty cans to stores and other locations around the state. Our MPCA research indicated this would result in more efficient recycling than having recycling bins such as we have today.

The bill went down to defeat as it had in 1971. A strong lobbying effort by the beverage industry, joined by the Minnesota AFL-CIO, and Governor Anderson's change of heart doomed the measure. The proposed legislation was introduced in successive sessions through 1983 but never passed. Perhaps if we had an initiative, like Michigan, whose constitution enables citizens to place a proposed law on the ballot, we could have succeeded as that state had.

Although the beverage deposit bill failed in the 1973 session, the Minnesota Environmental Policy Act (MEPA) passed (MN Stat. 116D). Governor Anderson was behind passage and his environmental staffer, Peter Gove, worked hard for the bill. MEPA requires environmental review for new projects, as well as for expansions of existing projects, environmental assessment worksheets, and environmental impact statements if the project has the potential for significant environmental effects. MEPA is second only to the Minnesota Environmental Rights Act (MERA) as the most effective environmental law enacted over the past forty years.

Early in February 1973 Governor Anderson met with the International Nickel Company (INCO) officials in New York. They told him that copper nickel ore mined in Minnesota would be shipped to Sudbury, Ontario, for smelting. Reporters called on me for comment,

101

and I pointed out that smelters at Sudbury are responsible for a high percentage of the sulfur dioxide emissions into the atmosphere of North America. I was quoted as saying, "We don't want to export our resources to add to the destruction of the Canadian landscape."

Soon I received a phone call from the Canadian Broadcasting Corporation radio headquarters in Toronto. They had read of my comment and wanted to interview me for their evening nation-wide program *As It Happens.* I agreed to be interviewed by a broadcast journalist whom I had heard many times—Alan Maitland. I repeated my concern about what would happen with copper nickel ore from Minnesota in the Sudbury smelters. Mr. Maitland was curious why a state official from Minnesota would be concerned about "adding to the destruction of the Canadian landscape." I told him I was a member of the Great Lakes Water Quality Board and that was one reason. But I also said I was concerned that Minnesota would be sending the ore to Canada for processing that would inevitably create more air pollution, not in the United States, where the mining occurred, but outside the country; it did not seem right to me.

A year later, I visited Sudbury and observed from a helicopter the moonscape caused by the enormous emissions of sulfur dioxide in the surrounding areas. The INCO and Falconbridge Company stacks during that visit in the summer of 1974 were emitting 4,400 tons per day of SO2, as I recall. The INCO "Superstack" was a towering 1,100 feet. Moreover, studies at the time showed that air pollution from this high smokestack was carried as far away from Sudbury as nine hundred miles, depending on the wind. Officials from the plants told me that plans were in progress to cut the amount in half within a few years. The amount today is approximately 220 tons.[34]

Beginning in 1975 a generic environmental impact statement on copper nickel mining in Minnesota was prepared, costing some five million dollars and taking three years to complete. By the time it was finished, however, copper and nickel prices had fallen drastically and INCO and another similar company, AMAX, were no longer interested in mining northeastern Minnesota deposits.

In the spring of 1973 we got word that state representative Neil Haugerud was introducing a bill to merge the MPCA with the Minnesota Department of Natural Resources. Regarding this as a burial in the DNR bureaucracy, we vigorously fought this idea. We were sure it would result in the PCA losing its independence, its effectiveness, as well as its citizen policy-making board. The governor seemed to be taking a "hands-off" position on Haugerud's bill.

We immediately received great public support for our fight against Haugerud's bill. Letters to the editor appeared around the state and a coalition of environmental groups rallied to "Save the MPCA." Both the *Minneapolis Tribune* and *Star* wrote editorials condemning the efforts to abolish the agency and transfer our functions to the DNR. The *Tribune* editorial stressed the openness of the MPCA as contrasted with the DNR, many of whose decisions "have been made in private." It also said, "One of MPCA's strengths has been its governing board, which meets in public." Similarly, the *Star* editorial explained "how a citizen board, meeting publicly, taking the testimony, weighing evidence and voting publicly, can put the spotlight on the hard pollution control questions facing the state." Both editorials pointed out the big differences in the duties of the DNR, which had a "split personality" with responsibilities for both promoting and regulating development of natural resources. The *Star* pointed out that the DNR was essentially a resource management agency whereas the MPCA was a "policeman of the waste that society discharges into the environment." The governor's "Loaned Executives Action Program" (LEAP) endorsed the agency as a "sound organization." Our LEAP executive was Douglas Dayton, of the Minneapolis Dayton family.

I was summoned to testify before a joint House-Senate committee and opposed the Haugerud bill on behalf of the agency. Citizens voiced considerable support for the PCA at the hearing, with several witnesses calling the PCA "the people's agency." When the measure was tabled, my deputy, Chuck Carson, flashed a "V" for victory sign at the audience full of people wearing "Save PCA" signs. Afterward I was pleased when a Republican House committee member from

Wayzata, Lon Heinitz, told me what a good job I did in defending the PCA actions. That hearing was the last we heard of the bill. Later Neil Haugerud and I often joked about his effort to "get our attention." Maybe that was what he had in mind. If so, he succeeded.

At the same time Senator Mel Hansen launched a legislative probe of my actions in setting up the Special Services Division of the MPCA, claiming that and other of my policies were "subverting legislative intent." I read Hansen's charges on the front page of the *Minneapolis Star* as I left the Minneapolis Convention Center on Saturday, April 8, 1973, where my family and I were attending the annual Sportsmen's Show. That was not too pleasant. As it turned out, we successfully disposed of Senator Hansen's attack at the same legislative hearing. Governor Anderson told me shortly afterward that I should be pleased with the outcome. I was, but was still a bit perturbed at having to spend the time and effort to fight off the attacks. Clearly, however, the fight showed the strong support we had throughout the state.

A very busy spring in 1973 also brought the Minnesota Experimental City (MXC) to the front pages. The legislature in 1971 had directed us to prepare an environmental impact study of the proposed Experimental City. An authority had been established by the legislature in 1967 with a board and executive director charged with planning a self-sustaining city of 250,000. The authority had the backing of Ford Motor executives, the American Gas Association, banks, foundations, and the University of Minnesota. It had narrowed potential sites to the Swatara area near Hill City, in Aitkin County, and a location outside Alexandria, in Douglas County.

Well before the hearing on this proposal I had been invited by Otto Silha, publisher of the Minneapolis *Star* and *Tribune*, and chairman of the authority's board, to lunch at the Minneapolis Club. He showed me the very impressive list of backers and argued that this would be a truly experimental city. I was aware that the concept was at least partially the brainchild of a professor at the University of Minnesota, Athelstan Spilhaus, who authored a widely syndicated weekly comic strip that appeared in the Sunday *Minneapolis Tribune*. After listening to Mr. Silha's explanation and arguments, I

At a Minnesota Pollution Control Agency meeting to vote on the Minnesota Experimental City proposal in 1973. Deputy Charles Carson is at far left, and to the right are MPCA members Marion Watson and Homer Luick. Photograph by Bill Bank, *Fergus Falls Daily Journal.*

told him that if the experimental city supporters could guarantee solar power for this city, I would support them. He could not, so we went ahead with our analysis of the environmental impacts and scheduled a public hearing at our boardroom.

When I returned from my meeting with Mr. Silha, I told Chuck Carson we would have a tough time beating them. Carson said he would organize the hearing, and he made contacts with people around Swatara and Alexandria. He was in regular contact with an attorney he knew in Fergus Falls, Dick Pemberton, who became a leader of the opposition and testified at our hearing. I recall getting to know one of the opponents from Swatara, Marie Rassier. She and her family were effective organizers. Strong organizing by Chuck Carson was the biggest reason for the result.

The MXC was scheduled to consume fifty-five thousand acres, largely farmland, which was a huge environmental negative in our analysis. Further, we foresaw the MXC drawing businesses and people from towns and cities up and down the western half of Minnesota, as well as the Twin Cities. In our judgment, this would suck the life out of many of those municipalities, causing significant economic and environmental problems. Spending millions on a huge new city could well lead to abandoning decaying cities.

Our board voted 8–1 to recommend to the legislature that the project be abandoned. Again, Governor Anderson was on the opposite side of the issue, but he did not react to the MPCA decision. My law school professor of practice and procedure, James Hetland, was on the MXC board and a vice president of the First National Bank at the time. He made some very sharp criticisms of the MPCA action at a news conference the next day, claiming that we gave the MXC "flippant consideration" and that we "undertook to play to the emotions of a small group of people." I told Dean Rebuffoni of the *Minneapolis Tribune* that the MPCA regarded Mr. Hetland's charges as "completely unfounded." The MPCA recommendation was accepted by the legislature and that is the last that was heard of an "experimental city" for Minnesota.

We Defeat Reserve Mining and Save Lake Superior

After that success, our attention quickly shifted back to the impending Reserve Mining trial. Once the asbestos issue became public news, the Reserve Mining controversy was much more intense around the state, and it quickly became a national news story. Between June 15 and the trial date set for August 1, there was no end of news. The *Minneapolis Star* reported on June 19, 1973, for example, that the MPCA was considering requesting that Reserve shut down the Silver Bay plant voluntarily to determine whether its discharges were related to the high concentrations of asbestos-like fibers found in Duluth drinking water. The MPCA board voted to request such a shutdown from July 22 to September 4 if such a link was found. This request was turned down by Reserve. The MPCA then authorized that a motion for a temporary shutdown be filed in court. The motion was taken under advisement by Judge Lord.

Sometime in this period of time, Jon Morgan and Ron Hays visited Reserve Mining at Silver Bay with Reserve's lawyer Ed Fride. While touring the plant, Ed Fride showed them a tank of recycling water containing the plant minerals. Fride scooped up several nearby minnows intending to prove that fish survive in the plant's effluent. Soon after he threw them in the tank, the fish jumped out and died! Fride said nothing and there was no need to, since his little experiment obviously failed.

As the trial began August 1, 1973, Mrs. Verna Mize of Potomac, Maryland, who grew up in the Upper Peninsula of Michigan, was outside the Federal Building in Minneapolis holding a large sign proclaiming "Lake Superior: Preserve it, Don't 'Reserve' It!" She had campaigned to stop the dumping for six years, writing literally thousands of letters to government officials and personally lobbying EPA chief Bill Ruckleshaus in Washington, D.C. She began her anti-Reserve lobbying three months before I did in August 1967, and it was not long before we collaborated in our efforts to stop the tailings dumping in Lake Superior. She became Minnesota's informal lobbyist in Washington. I kept in touch with her during my PCA days and thereafter even after Reserve finally stopped the dumping and went to Milepost 7 with its tailings in 1980. She lived a long life, dying on January 1, 2013, at the age of ninety-nine.

At the outset of the Reserve trial before Judge Miles Lord, Ralph Nader slipped into a back row of the courtroom. Lord spotted him and stopped the trial to recognize Nader. Nader had been following our work to stop Reserve's pollution of Lake Superior. Speaking to newsmen outside the courtroom, Nader said the case represents "the most demonstrable eco-catastrophe in the country." He went on to say, "Enough is now known to shut down the Silver Bay plant."

On October 24, 1973, John Hills, chief counsel for the federal government, produced a letter in trial from a Reserve official dated June 24, 1960, that showed that he believed rock samples from Reserve's Babbitt mine were asbestos. The Reserve official had written to James Gunderson, a geology professor at the University of Minnesota, asking his opinion. Gunderson replied on July 1: "The fragments you sent me are amphibole asbestos."

At the same day of trial, Ken Haley, Reserve's vice president for research and development, testified that Reserve had known for years that its discharges could cause the green water phenomenon in Lake Superior. This was in marked contrast with what Reserve's chief public relations official, Ed Schmid, had long told the public— that the green water was a natural phenomenon or an illusion.

During a break in the trial, in the fall of 1973, Judge Lord and the lawyers in the case, reporters, and company officials traveled to inspect Reserve sites and the tailings basin operated by Erie Mining Company at Hoyt Lakes. I was unable to go along because of a Prairie State and Canadian Province Energy conference in Banff, Alberta. It was there that I first learned of the plans to extract enormous amounts of oil from the tar, or oil sands, in northwestern Alberta. These are the oil sands that now produce a large percentage of the oil consumed in Minnesota and elsewhere in the United States.

In the meantime, Dr. Selikoff was studying body tissues from organs collected back to 1950 by local Duluth hospitals. Near the end of the trial, our counsel, Byron Starns, moved to join Armco and Republic as defendants. Judge Lord would not do it at the time, saying he needed more proof of their involvement in the pollution. So Byron then noted depositions requiring the chief executives William Verity of Armco and William DeLancey of Republic to produce their desk calendars to show that they were following earlier developments at Reserve. Judge Lord sat in on these depositions. The calendars showed that both owners were indeed deeply into following the case.

In the meantime, Ken Haley testified that Reserve had found that on-land disposal was not feasible. To the contrary, documents produced along with the desk calendars proved that Reserve not only believed on-land disposal was feasible but that Reserve had a plan to implement it. This infuriated Judge Lord, who felt that months of trial had been wasted and that Reserve had lied to him and the public. He promptly joined Armco and Republic corporations.

The trial neared conclusion after nine months. Byron Starns prepared charts for the trial showing how the fibers from the ore used by Reserve were identical to amosite asbestos. All three lawyers— chief counsel John Hills, Tom Bastow, and Starns—subpoenaed the economic and engineering records of Armco and Republic, following a suggestion by Judge Lord.[35] The cross-examination of the top officers of the parent corporations of Reserve Mining was revealing. Both the documents produced and the testimony of these officers showed how the claims by Ed Fride, going back to the enforcement conference, that Reserve could not have built the Silver Bay facilities at Babbitt because of a lack of water and land were false.

Equally significant was the revelation discovered in the Armco and Republic documents, now surfaced for the first time under pressure from the lawyers for the public agencies, that the parent companies had rejected Reserve's deep pipe solution and found a site for on-land disposal. Furthermore, the documents showed that by adding soda ash to the calcium chloride used in the transport of the taconite from Babbitt to Silver Bay a "zero-discharge system" was feasible. All this would result in *improved* profits for Reserve.[36]

As Tom Bastow concludes on these discoveries, "That night the evening news in Minneapolis reported the discovery of a 'massive corporate coverup.'" Immediately after this testimony, attorneys for Reserve, Armco, and Republic informed Judge Lord that they at long last would be willing to negotiate a settlement. The plaintiffs' negotiating team consisted of Donald Mount, Byron Starns, and me on behalf of the MPCA; John Hills and Tom Bastow for the federal government; representatives of the Minnesota Department of Natural Resources; the environmental groups in the case; and the other state governments that were parties to the lawsuit. Predictably, this went nowhere. In mid-April 1974, the lawyers for the team told Judge Lord that negotiations were stalled. After hearing that, the judge ordered the chief executives of Armco and Republic to his courtroom. They were questioned for three days by lawyers from Minnesota and Wisconsin as well as by Judge Lord. On the final day of trial, April 20, 1974, Judge Lord tried to wring from Armco's William Verity a commitment for on-land disposal and compliance with the MPCA air pollution regulation 17 for the stack discharges at Silver Bay. Mr. Verity refused the request and the judge put the finishing words on his decision and order that he delivered that afternoon.

My birthday party on February 27, 1974, with my three children: elder daughter Linda, son Steve, and daughter Carolyn.

Shutting down the plant, with its 3,100 workers, was such a momentous decision that when I was asked during a recess just before Judge Lord's decision if I thought the judge would in fact order the plant to close, I said no.

In fact, Judge Lord's detailed findings concluded that Reserve's "discharge into the water substantially endangers the health of the people who procure their drinking water from the western arm of Lake Superior." The judge then ordered that the discharge into Lake Superior be enjoined as of 12:01 a.m., April 21, 1974. The plant promptly closed in compliance with his order.

The courtroom was crowded that Saturday afternoon with over a dozen journalists, including national reporters, and the news of Judge Lord's decision went to all corners of the country. I recall a jubilant gathering of Minnesota environmentalists, which I joined, at the home of Rod and Naomi Loper in Minneapolis. They were active members of Clear Water Clear Air Unlimited, which supported the movement for on-land disposal of Reserve's tailings. During the evening at their home there were phone calls from around the state and nation cheering the decision by Judge Lord.

We got word the following Monday that Reserve had filed legal papers seeking a stay of Judge Lord's temporary injunction by the Eighth Circuit Court of Appeals in St. Louis. I had been fearful from the start that the Eighth Circuit Court would be reluctant to side with us if on-land disposal were ordered at the district court level. That was why the MPCA tried to reserve the right to proceed in state court in case things did not go our way in the federal courts, particularly the Eighth Circuit.

Ed Fride planned to argue the motion before a panel of that court's judges in Springfield, Missouri, where the judges were in a conference with the U.S. attorney general. I immediately chartered a Learjet to get our lawyers, myself, and Stan Strick, a *Minneapolis Star* reporter, to Springfield, Missouri, as fast as possible.

I could not help but think how my grandfather Alfred Merritt also had to face the Eighth Circuit in the appeal by John D. Rockefeller of the Duluth jury verdict that Rockefeller had engaged in fraud and misrepresentation in his dealings with the Merritts over the Mesabi Iron Range. In that case, the Eighth Circuit reversed and remanded the district court decision for a new trial, which Alfred Merritt and family could not afford, leading to a settlement for half of what the jury had decided.

The three-judge panel that consisted of Myron Bright, Donald Ross, and William Webster met in a small hotel conference room. They sat in their business suits behind a table covered by a green cloth. We sat behind card tables. As soon as this rather strange hearing was convened, I was taken aback by Judge Ross's calling on John Hills to make the first presentation. This was highly irregular since the hearing was on the motion by Reserve's attorney to overturn Judge Lord's ruling. Ross should have called on Fride first.

According to the account written by *Minneapolis Tribune* reporter, Bernie Shellum, who attended the session, during the brief hearing Judge Ross asked if there was evidence that "any individual has been harmed by this." My recollection was of more pungent language: "Show me the dead bodies on Superior Street [in Duluth] and we'll do something about it." Tom Bastow's book has it this way: "Show me one individual that's being harmed by this. Show me one dead body," Ross demanded.[37] Several months later while in St. Louis, for one of the many hearings that followed, I asked Clerk of Court Tucker for a transcript of the Springfield hearing from the tape recorder that was operating in the corner of the room. He curtly dismissed me, saying he "had more important things to do." I naturally concluded that the tape had been destroyed, à la President Nixon's tape with the blank gap in the Watergate case.

After the many hearings and briefs filed by the parties, Judge Lord's on-land decision was upheld by the Eighth Circuit Court in a lengthy and well-written opinion by Myron Bright. This was followed by a struggle by the parties to decide on the site for the on-land disposal. Hearings before a former Conservation Department commissioner, Wayne Olson, led to his decision favoring a site at Milepost 20. The Minnesota Supreme Court overturned this, and the site at Milepost 7 emerged as the final site. Milepost 7 is close to where Lax Lake is located. This location is where I originally favored a tailings basin. Governor Anderson and I agreed that this was the best site.

During the three years of the Reserve Mining case I saw Judge Lord many times in action both in his robes and otherwise. Well before the case went to trial, one Monday morning he arrived at my MPCA office in the Health Department and plopped a two-gallon glass bottle on my desk. He said he wanted me to "do something about this 'horse piss' being dumped next to my home on Christmas Lake." I said, "Judge, we will gladly look into this discharge." I then arranged to pick up the judge the following Friday afternoon in front of the federal courthouse in downtown Minneapolis. We drove to his home where he said he wanted me and the president of the lake homeowners association to proceed after dark to the horse barn and scout out the discharge. I said, "OK, I have the MPCA statutory right of trespass. Let's go. Aren't you going with us?" "Oh, no," he said. "I have my bib overalls here for you!" So the association president and I waited for dark before climbing the hill to the

Seated between James Dunlop, my public information director at the
MPCA (left), and Judge Miles Lord at Lord's Chanhassen home in 2012.

barn, where we discovered that indeed the yellow urine was ditched
and flowed right down to Christmas Lake. We reported back to the
judge and proceeded to follow up to end this pollution of one of the
cleanest lakes in the Twin Cities.

Judge Lord's momentous decision of April 1974 shutting down
Reserve may not have survived scrutiny by the Eighth Circuit Court
of Appeals in St. Louis, Missouri, but his permanent injunction calling for on-land disposal of the taconite tailings did. Ironically, the
Eighth Circuit judge Myron Bright, who wrote the opinion uphold-
ing Judge Lord calling for on-land disposal, died in December 2016,
as did Miles Lord, both of them in their midnineties.

My response to the media after Lord's April 20 order was that it
was "a courageous decision by a courageous judge—a history making decision. This wouldn't have happened but for the shocking
arrogance of the two companies, Republic and Armco." Jim Dunlop, my public information director at the MPCA, tells how he was
riding in the backseat of a car carrying Miles Lord in the right front

seat with Bob Mattson Jr., driving to the funeral of Don Boxmeyer, former reporter and columnist for the *St. Paul Dispatch* and *Pioneer Press*. On the way Jim says he told Lord "how much I admired him and that he was the bravest and most honorable judge ever." "Oh bullshit," Miles responded in typical fashion. "We all laughed!"

I think Jim was right on with that tribute. Miles Lord was the right Judge for the Reserve case. I think the fact that his colleague on the federal bench, Edward Devitt, was willing to hold Lord's temporary injunction over the heads of Armco and Republic Steel in order to decide the location of the on-land tailings basis shows the respect that so many of us have had for Judge Lord's handling of this landmark case.

During the appeal of the Lord decision, I attended most of the appellate proceedings before the Eighth Circuit Court of Appeals. On one occasion during a break I went to see Judge Gerald Heaney, the Eighth Circuit judge who had removed himself from participating in the Reserve case. We had a pleasant visit and he seemed pleased that I would look him up. Gerry Heaney and I went back many years to when I was the Eighth Congressional District chair of the Young Democratic-Farmer-Labor Party in Minnesota while attending the University of Minnesota Duluth in the 1950s. I had meetings with him in his home, which was near my home in Hunter's Park, Duluth, and also in his law office in the Providence Building in downtown Duluth. President Lyndon Johnson appointed him to the Eighth Circuit Court in 1966.

I had a lot of respect for Gerry Heaney's liberal views, his leadership of the DFL Party, and his stellar war record in World War II. He was an Army Ranger, who as an officer had led his unit up Pointe du Hoc during the Normandy invasion on D-Day. Having visited Pointe du Hoc many years later I can imagine the unbelievable courage it took to scale this almost forty-five-degree hill of several hundred feet under constant machine gun fire to reach the German bunker at the top. The bunker is still there. I never knew about Heaney's part in this heroic battle until shortly before his funeral in the summer of 2010. I attended his service at Holy Rosary Cathedral in Duluth. Sitting in the crowded sanctuary with Harry Munger, Willard's brother, I listened to trumpets from the balcony in back of the sanctuary playing Aaron Copland's beautiful *Fanfare for the Common Man*, which fit Gerry Heaney well.

Gerry Heaney and I differed on several occasions during my early days practicing law. A year after I began practice, he offered me a chance to return to my hometown and join his law firm in Duluth. I told him I was satisfied with the firm I was with in Minneapolis and turned him down. In 1969 after the Hotel Duluth MECCA hearing and before the first enforcement conference in May, my dad and I had lunch with Gerry at the Flame Restaurant on the Duluth waterfront near the Aerial Lift Bridge, which then stood at the current site of the Lake Superior Aquarium.

Some of what Judge Heaney said at that lunch disturbed me and led to some tension between us for a while. First, he tried to divert me from my leadership on the Reserve Mining case by urging me to do something "important" like sponsoring a large state program of $500 million for municipal sewage treatment plants around the state. I had no idea that he apparently had done legal or lobbying work for Reserve by that time, which likely was the reason he recused himself from the Reserve case later on. Naturally, I disagreed with him on this advice. Second, he said some unfortunate things about Chuck Stoddard, the author of the Stoddard Report, which had been released earlier in 1969. By this time I was very much a fan and friend of Chuck and vigorously defended him to Judge Heaney.

In his retirement, Chuck Stoddard wrote an excellent book titled *Looking Forward* in which he sets forth specific goals to meet the environmental crises we face. He says, "We have been warned long enough. We have a choice about the kind of world we leave to future generations. But unless we heed the warning signals, there may be no historian to recall one day that we failed to act in time."[38]

Reserve Mining stopped dumping taconite tailings into Lake Superior on April 15, 1980. After that date the tailings have been pumped

Minneapolis Star cartoon by Craig MacIntosh at the end of Reserve Mining's dumping of tailings into Lake Superior, April 1980.

nine miles away into the Milepost 7 tailings basin, which has become a large pond surrounded by dams. These dams prevent any overtopping and have functioned well ever since. When the plant was sold in the 1980s to Cliffs Mining Company, the production at Silver Bay (now called Northshore Mining) was reduced, fluctuating between six and eight million tons of pellets per year.

As a result the water balance at ten million or more pellets per year has been lost, resulting in too much water and plant tailings entering Milepost 7 than water taken from the tailings basin to make the pellets in the plant. Northshore had to build a treatment plant over by the Beaver River and discharge from there to the Beaver River, which runs downhill to Lake Superior. When this first occurred the company and the MPCA agreed on a maximum number of asbestos fibers of one million fibers per liter. Alden Lind of the Save Lake Superior Association led the effort, which resulted in the maximum reduced from the company figure of fifteen million fibers per liter to one million.

This maximum was later raised to six million fibers over the objection of the Save Lake Superior Association and individuals, including me. Although this amount is far from what went into the lake off the delta at Silver Bay, it still could be avoided if the company transferred production from one of its other taconite plants on the Iron Range to Silver Bay so that the water balance of ten million would be met.

CITIZEN ACTIVIST

From Public Servant to Private Practice

A year after Judge Lord's decision, and during the debate over where the tailings basin should be built, I decided to resign from my job with the MPCA. I had stayed much longer than I had planned and was anxious to return to private law practice. I had enjoyed most of my time as director of the MPCA, but I had pushed myself at top speed, figuring I wouldn't be there long. Since I could not rejoin my old law firm, I was glad to accept Governor Anderson's offer to do some part-time consulting for him on the Reserve Mining case. This enabled me to attend critical sessions and advise Wendy on what was happening. A very able young man named Peter Gove succeeded me as MPCA chief. He had been the governor's liaison with me, and we enjoyed a good working relationship over the prior three years. I was glad he took the job.

Before leaving the MPCA post the staff had a going-away gathering and gave me a unique present—a plaque with engraved depictions from *The Lorax*, by Dr. Seuss. The brass plate on the wooden tablet holding a copy of the book says, "For Persistence in Ridding the Once-Lers Amongst Us." I have treasured this gift and used the Lorax story in speeches many times ever since.

My four years and four months at the helm of the MPCA had been both exciting and wearing. Most of all I enjoyed the advocacy role on the environment that the job afforded as well as the chance to work with an outstanding group of folks who strived to change Minnesota's environmental policies and programs. That included an excellent staff of state employees and numerous citizens and groups around the state as well as nationally. I am grateful to Governor Anderson for the job and his support during the entire time I was there. When we disagreed, it was always with genuine respect for each other. It was an unforgettable experience. The support we received from the news media in Minnesota and elsewhere was key to the achievements of those years.

Finally, a brief tribute to my friend and boss, who passed away in July 2016. For some four or five years before Wendy Anderson died, I spent numerous hours with him talking over politics, golf, history, and fellow Minnesotans. I enjoyed these good visits and, of course, reminiscing about the past. Several times we drove around the Twin Cities in my Toyota, and during the first trips he repeated his aversion to Japanese cars. He held a grudge against Japan for what they did in World War II, and especially to several of his family members who died in that war. But he finally got over that topic. One day as we drove back from St. Paul he started talking to himself and said to the floor, not to me, that "it was the worst mistake I ever made," referring, of course, to his self-appointment to the U.S. Senate. He never blamed anybody but himself for the decision. I have thought how ironic it was that Wendy's decision to resign his governor's term made Rudy Perpich governor. If Wendy had not appointed himself to the Senate, Rudy Perpich may never have been elected governor. So it can be said that Wendy was responsible for Perpich becoming governor and serving the state of Minnesota for ten years. During those years Minnesota benefited from Perpich's strong support for the magnificent new History Center in St. Paul, one of the very best in the country.

Wendy had a quick mind and a good memory until it became clouded in his last years by what would likely have been termed "hardening of the arteries" in our growing-up years and dementia today. He liked reading history, especially of World War II. He kept up on the national news by religiously reading the *New York Times*, made available to him by friends who bought him a subscription. His bold support for on-land disposal of Reserve Mining's taconite tailings at Silver Bay not only pleased me, the Save Lake Superior Association, and the Minnesota Environmental Control Citizens Association, it also set the course for the Anderson administration on the environment. His many accomplishments over the many years he served the people of Minnesota will not be forgotten. In June 1975, he graciously acknowledged my contributions with a plaque that read:

> To Grant J. Merritt, Executive Director, Minnesota Pollution Control Agency
>
> In recognition of his selfless, courageous, and unwavering dedication to the protection of Minnesota's environment, which has helped so significantly to safeguard the well-being of the people of Minnesota.
>
> In grateful appreciation, Wendell R. Anderson, Governor

He presented the plaque to me at a special outdoor dinner at the backyard of the Governor's Residence on Summit Avenue in St. Paul on June 24, 1975. Almost one hundred of my friends were there that beautiful summer evening.

Right after the May 1975 announcement of my stepping down, I received a letter from Senator Hubert Humphrey, who wrote, "You have been a true public servant, constantly looking after the public interest and willing to take all the sticks and stones that can be thrown at you by the private interests. I congratulate you. You are entitled to the thanks of all of us."

I took the summer of 1975 to spend time with my family on Isle Royale prior to joining the law firm Nielsen, Blackburn and Merritt in Minneapolis that fall. I had a part-time contract to advise the governor on the Reserve Mining case. The consulting job with Wendy Anderson also enabled me to transition back to practicing law and,

With other state commissioners in 1975, with Governor Wendell Anderson at the podium. Photograph by Richard Olsenius, *Minneapolis Tribune*.

With my successor at MPCA, Peter Gove, at my going-away party hosted by Governor and Mary Anderson at the Governor's Residence in June 1975. Photograph by Supra Color, Inc., Minneapolis.

equally important, kept me involved in the closing chapter of the Reserve Mining case.

As such, I found myself once again in the courtroom on July 7, 1976, before Judge Edward Devitt, now the district judge handling the remaining Reserve issues after Judge Lord's removal from the case by the Eighth Circuit. The issue before Judge Devitt was the location of the tailings basin. The parties were not close to a decision. Devitt put the pressure on by instructing both sides to settle the issue. If they hadn't done so by one year from that very date, July 7, 1977, he said he would reinstate Judge Lord's injunction shutting down the plant once again. As we got up to leave, I noticed that William Verity, president of Armco, was in the row behind me. He recognized me and said, "Well, Merritt, you got what you always wanted." I looked him in the eye and said, "Mr. Verity, we did not set out to shut down the plant, just to get the tailings out of the lake."

During my time working as consultant to Governor Anderson, I enjoyed very good conversations with Tom Kelm, Anderson's chief of staff. He told me about a meeting at the Governor's Residence involving him, Wendy, and William Verity. After social pleasantries, they discussed where the tailings basin should be located. Verity said Reserve wanted to announce at a future date that they would go to the Lax Lake area but did not want to be blasted on that site like they had been by Governors Anderson, Lucey of Wisconsin, and Milliken of Michigan at a previous Midwest Governors' Conference on the Palisades Creek plan. Kelm told me that no deals were made at the meeting and that the company was told it would receive a fair hearing on its proposal. He also said the group discussed pollution control financing.

Over the next thirty-seven years I would spend a considerable amount of time working on environmental cases and causes, as well as handling regulatory matters in the transportation field. One such significant environmental case early on was on behalf of the Minnesota Conservation Federation versus the U.S. Army Corps

of Engineers in 1976. The issue was in regard to the corps's plan
to dredge the Duluth-Superior Harbor and dump the dredge spoils
(often referred to as "beach nourishment") out in the open waters
of Lake Superior. We were concerned that under this proposed plan,
pollutants in the dredged material would adversely affect the fish
and drinking water. The corps also planned to do more dredging in
the Mississippi River near the Twin Cities and dump the spoil into
the backwaters of the Mississippi River.

Milt Pelletier of the United Sportsmen of Duluth, a chapter of
the Minnesota Conservation Federation, hired me on the federation's behalf, and with the help of a new associate in our law firm,
Sam Myers, we sued the U.S. Army Corps of Engineers for an injunction to stop the dredging plan. The corps was represented by
Tom Larson, an in-house lawyer, who later joined the Briggs and
Morgan law firm and is still practicing there. The federal judge we
drew for the case was none other than Miles Lord.

We met for one of the court sessions in the Duluth Federal Building, the very building where my dad had the ground-level corner
office during his time as postmaster of Duluth. During the trial,
Judge Lord decided we needed to take a Corps of Engineers tugboat tour of the Duluth harbor. I recall standing in the pilothouse
as Lord imparted his knowledge of almost everything we passed in
the harbor. He also got in a few jabs at Judge Heaney, who lived in
Duluth. The two were mortal enemies, and I always said that whenever Judge Lord was in town and staying at the Radisson Hotel, the
sparks would fly between the Radisson and the federal courthouse
where Judge Heaney had his chambers.

The case was ultimately resolved with the Corps of Engineers
agreeing to find on-land sites for the dredge spoil both at the
Duluth-Superior harbor and in the Mississippi River. That ended
the "beach nourishment" plan.

Several years later I was hired to represent the Unimin Corporation in obtaining necessary environmental permits and approvals
for mining silica sand at Kasota, Minnesota, located on the east-
ern side of the Minnesota River across from the St. Peter area. Sam
Myers again assisted on the case, and we worked with a wonderful

Boarding the tugboat of the U.S. Army Corps of Engineers in Duluth during the Minnesota Conservation Federation lawsuit against the discharge of dredge spoils into Lake Superior in 1977.

lawyer from Le Sueur, Arthur Anderson, who always reminded me a bit of Dwight Eisenhower. We successfully went through the hearings on environmental impact and with the help of my friend Ron Hays presented a reclamation plan that would restore the land after the mining ended, and which is exactly what has happened. I have often cited this case to demonstrate that I am not anti-mining, as some have claimed because of my opposition to Reserve Mining's dumping at Silver Bay. In Unimin's case, I was pleased to represent a mining company that wanted to do everything possible to return the land to its previous state.

Early in 1982 I decided to make a run for the DFL nomination for the U.S. Senate seat held by Senator Dave Durenberger, the Republican incumbent who had defeated Bob Short four years earlier for the seat held by Hubert Humphrey.

I was taking on Mark Dayton, who was already well along with his campaign, and well financed with his own money. It was an interesting quest with a chance to chase votes around the state. At an event on the Iron Range where Mark Dayton, Eugene McCarthy, and I appeared on the platform together, I had a chance to tell a story about how in 1970 I had a meeting with then Senator Gene McCarthy in his Senate office in Washington, D.C., seeking his help on fighting Reserve Mining pollution of Lake Superior. He listened very well and commented that we would never allow that company practice now and when we finished he put his arm around me and said, "Just remember, Grant, it took Gifford Pinchot twenty years to accomplish what he set out to do." I went out of his office not quite sure what that meant but soon found out that Pinchot was the forestry advocate who persuaded President Teddy Roosevelt to set up the U.S. Forest Service, and then was appointed by Roosevelt to serve as its first director.

I had a good staff in manager John Harris, press secretary Jim Dunlop, and Tom Gale, who did research on issues like the Iron Nugget potential on the Mesabi, which has just now come to fruition. I soon realized, however, that I could not raise the kind of funds necessary to continue so I dropped out of the race in May 1982. Mark Dayton and I never went after each other and he won the nomination to take on Dave Durenberger but lost by about a hundred thousand votes.

In 1984–85, I represented a group of environmental groups, including Save Lake Superior, the Minnesota Environmental Control Citizens Association, and the Upper Peninsula Environmental Coalition, contesting the MPCA asbestos standard on discharges from Reserve Mining's Milepost 7 tailings pond. By this time the plant was not producing enough taconite pellets to achieve a water balance at the tailings pond, thus requiring a discharge from the pond into Beaver River, which flows south into Lake Superior. In other words, there is more inflow into the pond from precipitation than there was outflow to the plant for producing the pellets. If effluent was not drained out of the pond it would overflow the dams, which could ultimately threaten the city of Silver Bay. The company and the MPCA had agreed on an allowable limit of fifteen million asbestos fibers per liter into the Beaver River. We proposed that the limit be far less than that and ultimately we all agreed on a maximum of one million fibers.

In the course of this litigation, I recall arguing before a three-judge panel of the Minnesota Court of Appeals, chaired by Chief Appellate Court Judge Peter Popovich during which I used my small Dictaphone to record my oral argument. When I got back to my seat I set it down by my side but forgot to turn it off. When the tape reached the end it made a beeping noise, which the judge heard. He asked me if I had a recorder and I said I did. He ordered me to turn the tape over to the bailiff, which I did. He said I had violated a rule of the Supreme Court. I had never heard of any such rule. Further, there was a reporter with his camera recording the case in the corner behind me. Naturally, I was embarrassed, especially since many of the Silver Bay friends of Reserve Mining were in the audience. They could not help but snicker at my predicament.

The arguments were over shortly thereafter so I got in the elevator to go up to the court chambers. Judge Popovich then got on with me. I asked him how there could be a television camera recording the proceeding and I couldn't. He just laughed if off. I left with Milton Mattson from Save Lake Superior Association for lunch next door at the St. Paul Hotel; one of the Court of Appeals judges, Harriet Lansing, was having lunch nearby. I asked her about the supposed rule Judge Popovich had cited. She said she knew of no such rule and urged me to pursue the matter. So I did and found the rule didn't exist.

I subsequently made an appointment to see Judge Popovich. I explained there was no such rule preventing a lawyer from recording his argument and requested that he return my tape. He refused. Later, when he was about to become chief justice of the Minnesota Supreme Court, he issued new rules that included preventing such a recording. He sent me a copy and thereafter we laughed about the incident, which hadn't been so funny to me at the hearing.

Battling for the Environment in the Suburbs

During my early months at the MPCA, I had visited with the solid waste staff and learned there were some eleven hundred open burning dumps around the state of Minnesota. I went out to visit several of them courtesy of a DNR aircraft and pilot. They were filthy, often with rats living in the garbage. As I flew all around the state I saw smoke rising from these dumps. After my visits I could see why my solid waste director, Floyd Forsberg, favored phasing out these messy dumps. He was promoting what became known as "sanitary landfills," with a foot or so of clay liners and clay covers.

So we proceeded to close the dumps and replace them with landfills. My deputy, Chuck Carson, tried to amend the landfill rules to require four feet of clay under the landfills, but the opposition was too much for us. It wasn't long before these so-called sanitary landfills were leaking wastes into the groundwater and emitting noxious odors. They are definitely better than open burning dumps sending smoke up all over the state, but I sometimes wonder. The leachate from these landfills is anything but "sanitary" and often contains a deadly mixture of hazardous wastes such as the volatile organic compounds benzene and 1,1,2,2-tetrachloride (both cancer causing), trichloroethylene, methane gas, and others. By the mid-1980s landfill contamination was becoming a national crisis. In the late 1970s New York's Love Canal had highlighted the problem of the serious health issues caused by the large Hooker Company chemical dump. Homes and a school were built on the dump. Hazardous wastes from dumps were no longer "sanitary."

In 1987 I was hired by the Homeward Hills Homeowners Association (HHHA) to represent them in opposing the expansion of the Flying Cloud Landfill (FCLF), owned and operated by the Browning Ferris Corporation. FCLF was operated at first by Waste Management and then sold to BFI, which ironically was started in 1968 by Ed Drury, a garbage hauler from the Minneapolis area. The landfall is located next to the Minnesota River and marshy lakes in Eden Prairie across from the Flying Cloud Airport. It lies in what geologists call an ice kettle depression, a large sandy hole in the ground carved by the retreating glaciers. It was not a great site for a landfill, to say the least.

Perhaps the humorous idea, posited back in the 1960s by an Eden Prairie resident by the name of Grill, would have been better than the landfill on the bluff. He proposed that the city install four to six large airplane engines and let their propellers suck the smoke from an open burning dump at the bluff down the Minnesota River Valley. The engines would be mounted on wheels so they could move along the dump as it expanded. Of course, this novel idea never saw the light of day. Instead, Eden Prairie in 1970 was ready for a big celebration at the site of the newly permitted landfill. Miss America was there to cut the ribbon opening the landfill "while the local high school band played a command performance."[1]

I attended early hearings on the proposed expansion, which threatened residents to the east in the area of Homeward Hills Road and neighborhood. HHHA, one of the best homeowners associations I have represented, was headed by Susan Varlamoff, who proved to be a spirited and effective leader. She had the help of many of her neighbors and I was glad to work with them. During the next three years they held a blockade at the entrance of the landfill, a large "funeral procession" with seventy-five cars following a hearse with coffins to the capitol building in St. Paul, and many rallies, including a large one at Pax Christi Catholic Church featuring Lois Gibbs, the hero of the successful closure of Love Canal some ten years earlier.

State representative Sidney Pauly came to the aid of the group. She suggested that the city of Eden Prairie hire me as an assistant city attorney to work with Ric Rosow, a partner in the law firm that represented Eden Prairie. The city agreed, and Ric and I worked together on the project for approximately three years. I persuaded my next-door neighbor in New Hope, Minnesota attorney general Skip Humphrey, to recommend a contested case hearing to the MPCA. Susan and I met with the attorney general at his offices in St. Paul and Susan helped talk him into the recommended contested case hearing. A series of meetings with the MPCA staff and agency board finally resulted in the agency's ordering the contested case hearing.

This meant we would have a full-blown trial with witnesses and evidence before an administrative law judge.

The four issues formulated by the agency did not include the issue of fitness that we sought. That was a disappointment, of course, because we had compiled a fair amount of information to show that BFI was unfit. At the hearing held by the agency to consider whether to order a contested case, Roger Pauly, city attorney for Eden Prairie and Sidney Pauly's husband, spoke on the fitness issue in strong terms. He ended his speech by quoting a Boston BFI manager giving advice to his subordinate about the competition: "Put Kelley out of business, do whatever it takes. Squish him like a bug." Roger then added his own view: "Is this the kind of corporate citizen we want in Minnesota?" As a result of this hearing, the MPCA closed the dump, pending a decision on the expansion issue.

The hearings began on November 28, 1988, and concluded in the summer of 1990, with sixty actual days of trial plus motions and briefs. Administrative law judge Allan Klein heard the case. He was a highly respected judge and the brother of Blair Klein, whom I mentioned earlier because of his connection with Senator Gordon Rosenmeier, father of the MPCA.

Our chief adversary on the side of BFI was Chris Dietzen, who later became a Minnesota Supreme Court Justice. I first met Chris when he was a young lawyer, having recently moved here from the state of Washington. He was second chair to prominent attorney Robert Hoffman in a case involving a large development on Medicine Lake west of Minneapolis. Their firm, Larkin, Hoffman and Daly, represented the developer seeking to build a six-story apartment building on the little peninsula at the southeast end of the lake. I was hired by Minneapolis attorney Dick Gunn to assist him in opposing this proposal. So I was in the second chair across from second chair Chris Dietzen.

The trial was in the city council offices of Golden Valley. One day my witness was Dave Roe, president of the Minnesota AFL-CIO who lived right across from the proposed development. That morning I had read a fairly large ad in the *Minneapolis Tribune* by his organization criticizing environmentalists who were using environmental laws to oppose development. I spoke with Dave ahead of his testimony, naturally, pointing out that we better hope Hoffman or Dietzen hadn't seen the ad. Fortunately, they had not, and we went on to prevail in the lawsuit: the building was never built and the peninsula remains undisturbed. On several occasions since that case Dave Roe and I have laughed about that little episode.

Some twelve years later, in the BFI case, Chris was the lead lawyer and was assisted by another Larkin, Hoffman and Daly lawyer named Dick Nowlin. Scores of witnesses, including experts, were called to testify. The MPCA was a party, represented by Assistant Attorney General Dwight Wagenius. The organization Earth Protector, represented by Leslie Davis, participated in some of the hearings. During the summer of 1989 we went through a settlement mediation before Judge Phyllis Rhea, but this resulted in a stalemate.

Neighbors and others concerned about expanding the Flying Cloud Landfill testified together with expert witnesses whom we had called. In the fall of 1989, Judge Klein adjourned the hearing, directing the parties to negotiate a settlement. This created great concern among the Homeward Hills folks, and their fears were realized when a compromise settlement was reached between the city staff and BFI. The terms included monetary payments to nearby residents. The amount depended on how far they lived from the expanded landfill. A large payment by BFI to the city was also part of the offer. But before it went into effect it had to go before the city council.

The settlement infuriated Homeward Hills leaders, who started an all-out publicity campaign, distributing flyers throughout the city and placing ads in the two local newspapers and the *Minneapolis Tribune*. An outpouring of folks on our side resulted in lawn signs spread around the community and letters to the editor of all three papers.

BFI countered with large newspaper ads. The publicity and work by HHHA resulted in a large turnout at the hearings held by the city to decide whether to accept the large sum offered by BFI. The city council set three hearings at Pax Christi, Eden Prairie High School, and Wooddale Church in nearby Edina for late November and the last for December 12, when the council would vote whether to accept the deal.

Jerri Coller of the HHHA was the first of many citizens who spoke. She was vehement in her opposition to the cash settlement being offered by BFI. She implored the city to reject the offer. She said to the council, "Rarely in a person's life do they get the opportunity to make a difference in the world. You have this opportunity. Don't turn your back on it!"

Local firefighter Walter James came forward for the first time to describe the large fire that had occurred several years earlier at the Flying Cloud Landfill. He reported that "horrible plumes of dangerous clouds of heavy smoke and gases drifted over our neighboring city, homes, and families." There were "seven fire departments there for seven days, twenty-four hours a day," he said. On his third day of fighting the fire in the midst of the landfill, James was overcome by the gases and had to be hospitalized. The audience cheered this courageous member of Eden Prairie's firefighting team as he finished his speech.

There was a second hearing at the high school gym. Susan Varlamoff came back from Pennsylvania and testified. She referred to a visit she had with a Polish Solidarity leader who explained how the Polish people won with a "massive grassroots" campaign that swept the country, and she concluded that this "same story is being played out in Eden Prairie." Twenty-five speakers opposed the expansion and only six supported it. Three of them were from BFI.

Before the final and deciding hearing on the settlement offer took place, I was able to convince Governor Rudy Perpich to visit Eden Prairie for a tour of the landfill. Susan was able to postpone her return home to Pennsylvania so as to be there. HHHA arranged for the governor to arrive at Pax Christi Church to begin the tour. Father Tim Power welcomed him and after introductions we were off for a good tour on a cold day. Jerri and Susan rode with the governor in his chauffeured Lincoln. At the first stop looking out over the river valley below the dump, Rudy exclaimed, "This is one of the most beautiful spots in Minnesota."

Following the visit to the dump and vicinity, we drove to a park off Homeward Hills Road and found hundreds of people waiting to greet the governor. "Why the hell are we dumping garbage here?" he asked. He gave a short speech after being introduced by Jerri. Although he had another stop that Saturday morning, he was persuaded to come to the Coller home where we could sum up and have coffee. Dick Coller had a roaring fire going, and Rudy was glad to have some coffee. He was offered a fortune cookie; he had a good laugh with the fortune, which he read aloud: "Confucius says, 'Close the dump and you will have good fortune.' "

During the outdoor gathering, several residents had spoken about the dump problems and we had a chance to lobby the governor at the Coller home. Rudy explained how the MPCA had an independent citizen board that would not rubber-stamp anything, giving the benefit of the doubt to the environment. As he left he whispered to Susan, "Good job!"

After the governor departed, we sat around the fire, pleased with how the morning had gone and encouraged about our chances. And then it was back to planning for the next and last hearing on the settlement offer of BFI at Wooddale Church. Approximately four hundred people showed up. After some more speeches, the council was ready to vote. The motion to reject the settlement passed 4–1 with the mayor the only one voting for the expansion and cash settlement from BFI. So we were back in the hearings before Judge Klein. Much better news was coming in 1990.

The hearings continued until the summer of 1990. On August 1, 1990, as BFI drillers worked along the bluff overlooking the Minnesota River, some one hundred feet south and outside the landfill permit boundary, explosions and fires occurred at the drilling site. Since the drillers had found garbage along the bluff they figured the fires and explosions were due to methane gas from the garbage. The drilling crew had kept logs that showed the garbage was outside the permit boundary. When the landfill manager saw this he ordered the logs altered to say "fill." A new manager decided to investigate and discovered that the former manager had been told by the lab over the telephone that high gas levels were found along the bluff outside the permit boundary. When the manager heard this he told the lab not to send the test results to BFI, and the lab agreed. The results were sent four months later, however. The manager in March 1989 shoved the results in a drawer, where they remained until found by a BFI technician during the investigation in 1990. The results showed significant methane gas in the test borings taken in 1988 along the bluff.

On September 5, 1990, Dean Rebuffoni broke the news of falsified logs and suppression of evidence in the *Minneapolis Tribune*. This quickly led to capitulation by BFI. The company withdrew its permit application and requested dismissal of the contested case proceeding. BFI threw in the towel and that ended the eight-year battle.

Fighting a Virus in Lake Superior

Right after the Flying Cloud Landfill case concluded, I was approached by Floyd Anderson of Brooklyn Park on behalf of a small group of homeowners, including former wrestler Jesse Ventura, to represent them in opposing a developer who wanted to build in a wetland along West River Road near where the Izaak Walton League has a chapter house on the Mississippi River. We were successful in stopping this development and I got to know Jesse Ventura, who subsequently ran for mayor of Brooklyn Park and won. In a memorable statewide election in 1998, he was elected Minnesota's governor. I attended his first of ten inaugural events on a snowy January morning at the Izaak Walton chapter house in Brooklyn Park. The new governor was handed a bald eagle, which had been nursed back to health by the Raptor Center at the University of Minnesota. As Ventura held the eagle, with some trepidation, there was a yell: "Give us the bird, Jesse!"

After this case it was back to my general practice: motor carriers seeking new operating routes, or protecting existing ones; opposing the rerouting of Highway 55 next to Minnehaha Park in Minneapolis; fighting the general management plan of Isle Royale National Park on behalf of the Isle Royale Boaters Association; and opposing the construction of a large gravel pit at the Colvill area of the North Shore Drive east of Grand Marais.

During the four years when Gene Merriam was DNR commissioner (2003–7), a controversy arose over the Morehouse Park Dam on the Straight River in downtown Owatonna. The Minnesota DNR wanted to remove this dam, thereby lowering the level of the river upstream from the dam and enabling fish to move back and forth along the river where the dam was located. The dam extends back to the late 1850s and has produced power for grinding wheat into flour, and for a time was used by the Malt-O-Meal Company, which later moved to Northfield, Minnesota. The reservoir enabled skating on the Straight River and the dam became an icon for Owatonna, along with the famous Louis Sullivan–designed bank building in town.

In December 2002, the city council of Owatonna voted in support of the DNR proposal to remove the dam, which would have lowered the reservoir by several feet. This vote quickly energized large numbers of Owatonna residents and friends to campaign in favor of preserving the Morehouse Park Dam. I was hired by local businessman Chad Lange on behalf of the newly incorporated Dam Preservation Corporation to assist these residents in opposing removal of the dam. I researched the law on the rights of the riparian property owners upstream from the dam, and found a hundred-year-old Minnesota Supreme Court case, *Kray v. Muggli*, in which similarly situated owners above a dam had resisted removal of the dam that they had relied upon for over forty years.[2] The court held that the property owners had relied on the continuing operation of the dam and thereby had a right to its continuation. The owners had spent large amounts of money on improvements for boating, fishing, and other activities, and if the dam was removed they would have been "greatly injured and damaged in the enjoyment" of their property.

We held meetings with Mel Sinn, a staffer at the DNR, Commissioner Merriam, and representatives of the Minnesota Historical Society, who were receptive to working out a better result than the removal of the dam. As a result Doug Meyer, a retired engineer,

Dennis Von Ruden, president, and other members of the Dam Preservation Corporation, working with the DNR, designed a method of preserving the dam, adding a sixty-five-foot-wide bypass channel allowing for fish migration, and a seawall above the dam to reduce the speed of water flowing over the dam.

This solution was approved by the DNR in 2005 and in June 2006 the Owatonna City Council voted to approve the design. The Morehouse Park Dam was preserved. The local citizenry held a crowded celebration at the dam, which my wife and I attended.

In April 2007, I took on clients Izaak Walton League, W. J. McCabe Chapter, Save Lake Superior Association, and Trout Unlimited in litigation seeking to enforce federal regulations to protect Lake Superior from the invasion of the viral hemorrhagic septicemia virus (VHSV). This is a virus carried in the ballast water of saltwater ships entering the St. Lawrence River and then the Great Lakes that causes fish to hemorrhage. Ballast water carrying the virus is discharged into the lakes and then transferred to lake carriers taking on ballast water after unloading. This virus had invaded all the Great Lakes except Lake Superior at the time this litigation began in April 2008. It is only the most recent of the almost two hundred species that have invaded the lakes.

We sued the U.S. Department of Homeland Security and the Coast Guard, as well as the U.S. Department of Agriculture and its Animal and Plant Health Inspection Service on the grounds that they were not enforcing existing regulations. The rules would prevent vessels from taking on water for ballast from areas known to have infestations of VHSV.

My associate lawyer, Julie Root, and I argued that the general public would suffer substantial and irreparable injury unless these agencies promptly enforced their regulations. We sought a court order preventing the spread of the VHSV to Lake Superior. We alleged violation of the Minnesota Environmental Rights Act (MERA) on the basis that the defendants' failure to act rendered likely the arrival of the VHSV to Lake Superior and thus constituted pollution, impairment, or destruction of the natural resources of Minnesota.

The federal judge assigned to our case was James Rosenbaum.

He was appointed to the federal bench by President Reagan after serving as the U.S. district attorney for Minnesota. The defendants were represented by an assistant U.S. district attorney out of Minneapolis.

We alleged in three separate parts in our complaint that, even though there had not been actual injury, there was an imminent threat that the VHSV would arrive in Minnesota waters thanks to the continuous federal failure to enforce regulations already on the books. In the years since I began practicing law in 1962, federal and state courts are prone to dismiss cases so that they never reach the trial stage where the judges and juries can hear live witnesses and base their decisions on evidence.

In our VHSV case that is what happened. The U.S. defendants brought a motion to dismiss, arguing such issues as our standing to bring the case; whether the doctrine of "sovereign immunity" precluded going forward; and that the federal agencies' failure to act did not meet the requirement of *Heckler v. Chaney* (470 U.S. 821 1986), in which the Supreme Court held that Congress must have set standards governing the agency's discretion in order to bring a lawsuit.

Judge Rosenbaum rejected our contentions on all these issues. With regard to our legal standing to bring this lawsuit, he admitted that we had the "care and concern" for Lake Superior, but he questioned whether our concern was "concrete and particularized" enough. He said, "Plaintiffs are not concerned about VHSV's presence in Lake Superior and its fish population. They are concerned the lake might become infected in the future. To date, there is no evidence VHSV is in Lake Superior as opposed to the other Great Lakes."[3] He went on to state: "Absent VHSV, there is no actual harm. And absent actual harm, plaintiffs must allege imminent harm. . . . Fatal to their claim, they have failed to do so."

Thus the main basis for Judge Rosenbaum's dismissal of our case was wrong. We *did* plead imminent harm to Lake Superior. And we were vindicated in our belief that the virus would shortly arrive in Lake Superior waters by the actual arrival of VHSV shortly after the judge ruled against us.

After the order dismissing our case, we decided there was no use in seeking review by the Eighth Circuit because of the pervasive right-wing composition of that court. Instead, we filed a motion before Judge Rosenbaum to have him correct his order. We argued that we did indeed plead "imminent harm"; that he should renounce his statement that there may be an "antiviral agent" stopping the introduction of the VHSV into Lake Superior; and finally that he should revise his decision on standing to reflect that ten months after his order VHSV was discovered in Lake Superior.

The judge had raised the possibility of an "antiviral agent" in the lake during our oral argument. He suggested that the presence of taconite tailings in Lake Superior might have been the reason VHSV had not yet arrived in the lake. I thought he was kidding!

To be fair to Judge Rosenbaum, he is not different from federal judges around the country who preserve the federal courts' limited jurisdiction when it comes to suing federal or state agencies. I ran into this when I sued the National Park Service, contesting the general management plan at Isle Royale National Park, and when I sued the Department of Transportation contesting the Highway 55 reroute in Minneapolis near Minnehaha Park. In both cases, I argued the agencies were acting in an arbitrary and capricious manner. There are exceptions to the jurisdictional rules, but they are difficult to prove before federal judges. This is obviously an area where Congress needs to act so that citizens are not frozen out of the courts when they present evidence of arbitrary behavior by federal agencies.

But the fact remains that Judge Rosenbaum made a fundamental mistake in our lawsuit that permeates his handling of the issues of the case—he somehow overlooked the three separate places in our complaint where we did plead imminent harm. And worse than that, he would not admit his mistake when we asked him to do so after the case concluded. Furthermore, he claimed in his order disposing of our post-trial effort that correcting his mistake "would wholly redefine the substantive rights of the parties." If that were true, perhaps he would have decided in our favor, which he clearly did not want to do. Granting our motion would have merely corrected his mistake but would not have changed the outcome. Nor would it have allowed an appeal to the Court of Appeals, as we had earlier decided not to appeal. That said, the judge claimed in his order denying our motion that we were somehow trying to appeal, which was also a mistake by the judge since the time to appeal had long passed.

Such is the way litigation in the environmental field goes at times. A major lesson of this particular case is that the field of administrative law should take a closer look at the deference afforded administrative agencies and their "expertise." This doctrine has been sacrosanct now for over sixty years. I first encountered it in graduate school in public administration at the University of Minnesota in 1955–56, later in law school, and during my practice of motor carrier law. The idea is that the courts should show proper deference to the administrative agencies because of their "expertise." This is, in general, a sound rule. Administrative agencies are staffed by public servants who are specialized and more knowledgeable than judges about specific subjects. But what if the case is not based on an agency's special knowledge but instead on its reluctance to enforce its own rules? That can happen either because of fear of the interests who might have to spend money to comply or because the agency has buckled to the pressure of special interests—which happens more than one would like to believe. In this case we don't know why the Departments of Homeland Security and Agriculture failed to enforce their duly adopted rules. We do know that if they had done so, the presence of VHSV in Lake Superior could well have been avoided.

Parks and Trails

In the autumn of 1994, I heard that the new Grand Portage State Park was being dedicated at the state's largest waterfall. So I donned my voyageur's sash, belt, and cap with tassel, and headed to Grand Portage. I had not worn this regalia since being inducted into the Order of the Voyageurs at a small lake north of Crane Lake back in my PCA days. Upon arrival I met Bill Buell, who was there with his wife, Ginny, their two children and their friendly dog. After getting acquainted with them, Bill told me about the organization now known as Parks and Trails Council of Minnesota (PTC). He invited me to join. I agreed and have been a member ever since, serving as a board member from 1995 until 2009 and president from 2004 to 2007.

One of the joys of my life has been my involvement in the council. Since 1954 it has been acquiring, protecting and enhancing critical lands for public benefit. The first president was State Supreme Court Justice Clarence Magney, who also served as mayor of Duluth and owned a cabin on Lake Superior at the Caribou River. He and several other pioneers of parks in Minnesota—Reuel Harmon, Sam Morgan, and Tom Savage—had the idea of acquiring land and then turning it over to the Minnesota Department of Natural Resources at appraised value for parks and trails. This concept has been carried on to the present day. There is the risk, of course, that the state could decide not to buy, or that the DNR appraisal would be less than the council paid for the property. That has rarely happened because the council has kept in close touch with the needs and goals of the DNR.

The largest project, beginning in 1997, raised a million dollars from contributors to add the Gold Rock property to the Split Rock State Park. The eighty-one-acre Gold Rock property was owned by the Congdon family in Duluth and included thirty-seven hundred feet of frontage on Lake Superior. There are numerous other examples of acquisitions either within state parks or adjacent thereto to enhance the enjoyment of already established parks. On some projects we started from scratch.

I was fortunate in that project to be approached by Howard and Sherry Burgdorf, who had purchased a sizable tract of Lake Superior shoreline east of Split Rock State Park from Sam and Helen Mayo, critics of Reserve Mining. The Burgdorfs became good friends of my uncle Milton Mattson of East Beaver Bay and the founder of Save Lake Superior Association. After the Burgdorfs became owners of this magnificent property, they took Milton up to the high point of their new ownership, above the scenic North Shore Drive, where on a clear day you can look across the broad reach of Lake Superior to the Wisconsin shore, and look down on the Split Rock Lighthouse. Milton, who was not prone to speak in superlatives, said, "This is the most beautiful view of Lake Superior I have ever seen."

The Burgdorfs asked me if the Parks and Trails Council would be interested in buying their property. We were able to arrange a purchase. Their cabin and much of the shoreline was conveyed to Craig Blacklock, son of Les, nationally recognized photographer, and a well-known photographer in his own right. Craig Blacklock has dedicated this property to the memory of Nadine Blacklock, former president of PTC. The rest of the land was sold to the park. In 2004 the PTC dedicated a plaque, created by the artistic talent of Howard Burgdorf, which contains an engraving of Milton that is now firmly part of the view that Milton liked so much. It is my hope that someday soon the DNR will build a suitable road or trail to the "Milton Mattson Overlook," as we call it, so the public can enjoy the view.

I have enjoyed many pleasant trips on behalf of PTC to attend meetings at many of our parks and trails. In recent years, we have learned the importance of hiking, biking, and other outdoor activities to good health and that has spurred more interest in park and trail use. My predecessor as president, Jeff Olson, said, "Our state parks are extraordinary health and fitness clubs with numerous special amenities." The increasing Minnesota population has also resulted in more visitations. Friends and groups have been instrumental in promoting and maintaining many of our trails and parks. The PTC has been fortunate in raising funds to add land to parks and to build trails. It is a continuing task. Over thirty-two hundred members have made generous gifts to PTC over the years. By acting as a bridge to the DNR, we are able to save many acres that otherwise would be developed.

A dream of mine is related to the Reserve Mining site at Silver Bay. A large delta of over three hundred acres was formed from the dumping of taconite tailings into the lake south of the taconite plant. In 1986 the state of Minnesota accepted ownership of the delta in order to convince a new company, Cyprus Minerals of Colorado, to buy the Silver Bay operations from Reserve and resume production. Since the state now owns the delta, it is my view that the public should be allowed to hike and use the space, which has a memorable view of Lake Superior. Access could be provided with trails, picnic areas, and camping facilities. The dust problem from the stacks at the plant site would require more abatement control and enforcement. The MPCA would have to make sure there is no health risk from walking on the bed of taconite tailings. The history of the plant and the egregious dumping of sixty-seven thousand tons of tailings per day for years into Lake Superior should be made known to visitors.

Parks and trails cannot flourish without attention to environmental regulation. Carbon dioxide emissions are warming the globe. Lake Superior waters around Isle Royale are much warmer in July and August than a few years ago. The wolves at Isle Royale are in a crisis with the park service considering various options to restore the population. Only a long-term reversal of the warmer climate, with a return of periodic ice bridges between Canada and the island, will allow the wolves to cross over from Canada, as they did in the 1940s and in 1997. In 2007 ice bridges occurred from the Black Bay area across the lake in Ontario to Blake's Point and again in 2014 between Isle Royale and Grand Portage.

Recognizing Progress—and Staying Alert

Has the environment improved since the movement took off in the late 1960s? We won some big battles after the environmental movement began to come alive in the mid-sixties, so my answer is yes. In Minnesota we today have a cleaner Lake Superior, having stopped the dumping of those huge amounts of taconite tailings at Silver Bay. We have better soil and groundwater with the closing of some thousand open, burning garbage dumps. There is less smog hanging over the cities. The massive federal and state expenditures on sewage treatment plants and requiring tertiary treatment at some of those plants have had a positive impact on rivers and lakes. We have had a de facto and then a legal moratorium in Minnesota on building any additional nuclear power plants. Nationally, we have better laws to reduce pollutants from impairing our air, water, and landscapes. The Environmental Protection Agency has been successful in setting national standards and in many enforcement actions around the country.

David Zwick, who founded Clean Water Action in 1972, recently pointed out the "big difference in point source pollution" since passage of the Clean Water Act of 1972. There has been significant reduction in those sources, which are the large industrial and municipal dischargers. He cited the progress in the seventies and eighties after the lawsuits in which the U.S. Supreme Court struck down President Nixon's impoundment of sewage treatment funds appropriated by Congress.

Zwick also says that "nonpoint source pollution abatement has lagged far behind point sources." The "period of rapid progress" dried up in the 1980s with the slowdown occurring under President Reagan. The major nonpoint sources in Minnesota are farms with runoffs of sediment, fertilizer, pesticides, and herbicides. Clean Water Action has become a unique national environmental group that focuses on electing state and national politicians who will work on environmental issues. A good example is Chris Van Hollen, elected in 2002 with the strong support of Clean Water Action to the U.S. House from Maryland's Eighth Congressional District. Van Hollen steadily rose to the top ranks of House Democrats, served as chairman of the Democratic Congressional Campaign Committee, and was elected to the U.S. Senate from Maryland in 2016. I served many years as a member of the Minnesota board of Clean Water Action and later the national board of directors from 2000 to 2005.

Forward progress has resulted from laws such as the National Environmental Policy Act, and its state versions, which have adopted the "look before you leap" approach to new industrial expansion. Environmental impact statements have been successful in controlling and even avoiding new sources of pollution. If we had had such laws earlier, we may have avoided the problem of how to dispose of radioactive fuel rods from nuclear power plants. Nuclear power plants promoted by the Atomic Energy Commission in the years 1946–70 did not generate environmental impact studies or citizen activists raising protests about the failure of the government and the utilities to deal with the disposal of radioactivity from the reactors.

If we had had NEPA laws back in the days before the environmental movement gathered force in the late 1960s, perhaps the dumping of huge quantities of taconite tailings into Lake Superior would have been avoided. The same thing could be said about allowing invasive species to be carried in ballast water by saltwater vessels and lake freighters throughout the Great Lakes.

Even with good environmental review laws in place, it still takes an alert citizenry, as well as a strong and responsive government, to make sure the laws are enforced. The growing concern about the hydraulic fracturing of rock now occurring all across the country in the massive underground shale formations is the result of exempting development in drilling for natural gas from the federal environmental protection laws. This happened in the early years of the George W. Bush presidency. As a result, there are serious questions now after drilling is well along about water pollution of vast groundwater supplies and nearby wells as well as air pollution effects from the ongoing "fracking." In addition, huge quantities of water are mixed with frack sand and chemicals, including volatile organic contaminants such as benzene. All of this should have been analyzed before the drilling began and proper permits required.

One of the advances of the past forty-plus years is the advocacy of individual citizens and activist groups when a pollution problem arises. Examples are the citizen campaigns to deal with the health issues from contamination at Love Canal; stop taconite tailings from flowing into Lake Superior; and close the Flying Cloud Landfill and halt the expansion of that landfill sought by Browning Ferris Industries.

Another lesson learned from my environmental activity over the past fifty years is that an alert citizenry should not wait until definitive evidence is available to act in abating pollution. When we began in 1968 to stop Reserve's dumping of taconite tailings directly into Lake Superior, we had enough presumptive evidence to save Lake

Superior. We had evidence from many commercial fishing families along the north and south shores that their nets were clogging up with the tailings from Silver Bay. And they told us that the fishing for herring and lake trout had dropped off drastically because of the tailings. We had the evidence of airborne tailings at homes such as that of Mrs. Edel Schneiderhorn in East Beaver Bay some two miles west of the Silver Bay plant. We also knew from her that Ed Schmid, the public relations vice president of Reserve, told her that these windowsill deposits were from the ore boats out on the lake. She asked him, "How could that be since it was February and no such ore boat traffic had passed by since December?"

Further hoodwinking by the company related to the green water that we saw flowing from Silver Bay toward Duluth and Wisconsin. Reserve called the green water an "illusion." When we started efforts to change what was happening at Silver Bay we did not have all the evidence produced later at the trial before Judge Lord. We did not yet know of the public health threat from the fibers in the tailings that proved to be virtually identical to asbestos. By January 1969, however, we had the Stoddard Report, which established that Reserve tailings were found in Wisconsin samples from Silver Bay.

In short, we had plenty of reason to call for action before all the science was in. The environment clearly was threatened, and good public policy demanded strong action to stop the dumping. One could pass by the Reserve plant by either car or boat and see the huge pollution going on. No other taconite company was allowed to do this. The tailings that were being dumped on the large delta created by previous dumping were sliding gently off the delta into Lake Superior. We could easily see that Reserve's long-standing claims that the tailings were discharged to the lake by a heavy density current that carried them to the bottom of the "great trough" outside Silver Bay were just more hoodwinking. This lesson should be applied to the current debate over whether climate change is caused by humans. The time is now to take action to reverse the causes. We have sufficient evidence to take action now. Fortunately, we are beginning to do so. However, we still have naysayers who want more evidence that humankind is chiefly responsible. We should not wait for more evidence; there is plenty of that already, just as there was in the Reserve Mining case back in 1968.

One of the unsung heroes of the environmental struggle to stop Reserve's dumping of tailings in Lake Superior was Milton Mattson, operator of a general store in East Beaver Bay. Milton took a courageous stand in favor of on-shore disposal of Reserve's tailings and it cost him dearly. Not a few people from Reserve Mining Company, and their sympathizers, boycotted his store for years because of his quiet but firm opposition to Reserve's degradation of Lake Superior.

My experience these past forty years with two governmental models that encourage citizen participation in solving environmental problems convinces me that we need much more of this. The first is the idea of a citizen policy-making board such as the one legislated by Senator Gordon Rosenmeier for the Minnesota Pollution Agency in 1967 and signed by then governor Harold LeVander. It proved its worth for thirty years, until the board was downgraded in 1997 by Commissioner Charles Williams serving in the administration of Governor Arne Carlson.

During those thirty years, the citizen board made good decisions in the open. The legislature thought it was a good idea to have the MPCA evaluate the Minnesota Experimental City concept and that led to the end of that "utopian scheme," as board member Steve Gadler referred to the MXC during the public hearing. Gadler was a Republican appointed by the Republican governor Harold LeVander. Senator Rosenmeier was a staunch conservative. Consequently, the idea of having citizen boards invested with policy-making authority, instead of serving, as so many other boards, in an advisory capacity, is not a partisan matter. In fact, when I visited with Arne Carlson about eight years after he left office about the downgrading of the MPCA board, he said he didn't like advisory boards. I said this was no such board and he was surprised.

Having served the MPCA citizen board for over four years, I am a strong advocate for this type of governmental structure. It has many advantages. First, it brings citizens into the arena of decision making. They are given an opportunity to express their views in an

At Taconite Harbor on Lake Superior in 1995, twenty years after I had left the Minnesota Pollution Control Agency.

open meeting and advocate for their positions directly to the decision makers. That is not always possible with an agency whose commissioner makes all the decisions. At the MPCA, during the thirty-year period after the agency began in 1967, the executive director recommended the staff position and the board weighed that together with the public input in making its decision.

When I was executive director, we held many public hearings before making the recommendation to the agency board. I recall how on several occasions, board member Steve Gadler would ask my deputy director, Charles Carson, during agency meetings: "When is the public hearing?" So the public often had two chances to be heard if a public hearing was held before the agency board meeting. What this did, of course, was to open up the issue to the public because the media got involved, and that resulted in better decisions. As a result of citizen input and a good staff, we challenged the status quo by public actions and with public hearings. We reached out to more citizens through the intense media coverage of the agency, resulting in public understanding and support for our actions. In addition, we reached out to Minnesotans across the state through our district offices. When they were established, the new district directors were charged with making contacts with residents in their districts in order to carry out our environmental mission.

Although the MPCA in the 1970s had to sue some corporate polluters and recalcitrant public entities, most of the disputes over compliance were settled amicably by negotiated settlements called stipulation agreements. At times we would extend the time for compliance when warranted with time variances. The only time I would disagree with Steve Gadler was over these time variances that I sometimes recommended. Steve voted against all variances whether time extensions or substantive variances. There were occasions when we had to lock horns with other state agencies. On one memorable occasion we sued the Minnesota Highway Department for operating a black-smoke-belching asphalt machine on the state highways in violation of our air pollution regulations. That lawsuit quickly led to a stipulation agreement between Highways and the MPCA that stopped that polluting source. And that was not the only time we had to confront other state agencies like the Health Department, which supported nuclear power plants. Another example was over the location of the Grand Portage Hilton Hotel as described in the preceding chapter. In that instance we had to oppose friend Jim Heltzer, commissioner of economic development, and the governor in order to move the hotel away from Raspberry Point next to Lake Superior. And we had to vigorously oppose the DNR right after I started work for the PCA when the DNR tried to sidetrack our on-land solution for the taconite tailings being dumped into Lake Superior.

Another advantage of the MPCA model of a state administrative agency is that the staff director must promptly take the controversial issues confronting the agency to the board, rather than letting them sit on his or her desk, which results in a more efficient handling of public business. Without a forthcoming board meeting, a commissioner may be tempted to let a hot controversy simmer for weeks or months.

Congressman John Blatnik and Ed Fride criticized me because I relied on North Shore fishermen in the Reserve case rather than on engineers and other witnesses with expert degrees, most of whom worked for Reserve. When asked about this by Ed Fride under oath, I said, "And I think that many of the Norwegian-Swedish-Finnish fishermen along the shore and old citizens that know a great deal what's going on are people with common sense who often times know the facts and are entitled to be listened to. And I certainly don't subscribe to the view of any elitist philosophy that we listen only to experts, Phds or otherwise."[4]

We did not have all the evidence produced later at the trial before Judge Lord. We did not yet know of the public health threat posed by the fibers that were found to be virtually identical to asbestos. From the Stoddard Report we knew by January 1969 that Reserve tailings were found in Wisconsin waters of Lake Superior. In short, we had plenty of reason to call for action before all the science was available.

Unfortunately, the roles of the commissioner and board members changed in the mid-1990s by Charles Williams, MPCA chief under Governor Arne Carlson. Working with the governor's office, Williams proposed changing the Rosenmeier structure of the agency by demoting the role of the citizens board and making the commissioner a voting member and chair of the board. Several board members attempted to stop these changes in the legislature but were muzzled by the governor's chief of staff, Morrie Anderson, who sent the board members a memo on February 28, 1995, admonishing them to support Williams's legislative proposal. The memo said, "Governor Carlson expects full cooperation by his appointees with this initiative and expects that you will give Commissioner Williams your full support as he and his staff seek legislative approval." The changes were passed by the legislature, signed by Carlson, and the MPCA has not functioned since then as it did in its first thirty years. Jim Dunlop, who was a member of the board for three years during the succeeding Ventura administration, described to me an incident when he had voted against then commissioner Karen Studders on a feedlot issue and thereafter was questioned by Studders as to why he didn't support the staff. He told her that the role of the board is often to side with the citizens appearing before the board and not necessarily follow the staff input. The legislature abolished the citizens board in 2015.

The second example of a government model that encourages public participation was the enforcement conference procedure that brought the Reserve Mining case to public attention in a big way. The Lake Superior Enforcement Conference was one of over fifty such conferences convened under the Federal Water Pollution Control Act during the 1950s and 1960s. The Reserve proceeding had six separate public hearings over the period May 1969 through April 1971.

The Lake Superior conference was a huge success in arousing the public to fight the vast pollution of the Big Lake by Reserve Mining. Because the protagonists were front and center, and the dumping so clearly wrong, the public began the long campaign to right the wrong. Active environmentalists led the way with the media playing a large role in arousing the public to action in getting Reserve on land. We cannot forget the actions of the memorable Charles Stoddard. His five-federal-agencies report triggered the enforcement conference proceeding and action leading to the trial before Judge Lord. He withstood savage attacks by Reserve, as well as federal and state officials. As Congressman Bruce Vento, St. Paul, put it, "He made a significant contribution to the quality of life of his fellow Minnesotans and all Americans. . . . The values and integrity that guided his decision and work reflect well upon the purpose of public service and the impact a good man can make." This reflection upon Stoddard's life was contained in the obituary written by the environmental reporter Dean Rebuffoni in the *Minneapolis Tribune* of December 30, 1997, after Chuck died in Wisconsin at eighty-five. Vento had the obituary printed in the Congressional Record of March 26, 1998. It contained a quote from me: " 'Chuck Stoddard was a fearless public servant,' said Grant Merritt, a Minnesota conservationist who played a key role in the campaign to end

Reserve's discharge into Lake Superior. 'Chuck did his job regardless of the heat he had to take,' Merritt said. 'The Stoddard Report gave us the scientific basis we needed to seek on-land disposal of Reserve's tailings.' " That report was proof that the tailings were observed in Wisconsin waters over toward Bayfield.

Unfortunately, Congress repealed the enforcement conference provisions of the federal law, shortly after the Reserve case went to litigation, and the law now relies on provisions allowing EPA to go directly to court. Without the strength of an aroused public opinion, it is often less likely that federal or state officials will have the support to sue the polluters. Success in the Reserve Mining case shows developing public opinion played a large role in the eventual on-land solution for the taconite tailings. "Did Taconite Save the Iron Range?," an article by D. Perry Kidder in the spring 1989 issue of the Minnesota Historical Society magazine *Roots,* concluded: "One legacy of the thirteen-year Reserve controversy is that it served as a catalyst for increased organized citizen activism. . . . The new environmentalists' greatest bequest to us was the preservation of the priceless heritage that is Lake Superior."[5]

Also important is the increased citizen action involving the Minnesota Environmental Rights Act, the single best environmental statute of the past forty years, and the successful blocking of BFI's proposed expansion of the Flying Cloud Landfill. Governor Anderson said it well in a special message to the legislature on March 3, 1971: "From now as far into the future as we can see, we must protect and preserve. . . . The fight will last as long as man remains in Minnesota." We will need advocates from the citizenry and within government for years to come in order to restore, protect, and preserve our environment. Citizen participation in policy-making decisions is the key. Abraham Lincoln said in his first debate with Stephen Douglas in Ottawa, Illinois, on August 21, 1858, "With public sentiment, nothing can fail; without it nothing can succeed." In order to make that possible, it is crucial to let the public know what is going on.

Sometimes, however, letting people know what is going on can get you in trouble. The painful aftermath of my prominent highlighting of the NSP incident involving the MPCA nuclear power plant regulations is one example. Another goes back to my newspaper delivery boy days in 1945. One day, when turning in my paper collections at the *Duluth News Tribune* offices, I told my manager that I was getting tired of delivering Ridder's Nazi newspaper. This comment, of course, nearly cost me my job. The manager called my mother to tell her that I better lay off that talk or I would be out of work. I guess I thought the newspaper employee should know about the trial in New York, which I heard about from my dad, who brought home the New York–based *PM* newspaper, which was reporting on *Foerster v. Victor Ridder et al.* The case began after a professor, Friedrich Foerster, had made public statements during World War II alleging that "Victor Ridder was a Nazi sympathizer doing Hitler's work in the United States." Ridder countered, claiming Foerster "distorted the truth." Foerster sued Ridder for libel. Victor was the patriarch of the Ridder family, owners of ten newspapers, including the *Seattle Times*, the *Journal of Commerce*, the German-language newspaper *New Yorker Staats-Zeitung und Herold* and the *Duluth News Tribune* and *Herald*.

Foerster was represented by a great trial lawyer, Louis Nizer. The trial was fascinating for the meticulous cross-examination by the masterful Nizer. The evidence proved that Victor Ridder, and his brothers Bernard and Joseph, were close allies of Adolf Hitler and couriers of Nazi propaganda during the thirties and World War II, and that Victor was Hitler's "Unterführer" representing Germany in the United States. Nizer recapped the evidence in his book *My Life in Court* in a fifty-nine-page chapter that contains long passages from the transcript. The jury found in favor of Foerster and awarded him damages.

I learned that I should watch what I say, however. I also learned how news of an important event such as this trial could be a front-page story in a New York newspaper and on the classified ad page buried in the back of the *Duluth News Tribune*. This trial undoubtedly played a role in my interest in handling trials as a lawyer and perhaps my decision in the summer of 1959 to attend law school.

The adversary system of our American jurisprudence is the world's best method of delivering truth and justice, so long as the litigants abide by the rules and are honest. The Reserve Mining and Flying Cloud cases both exemplify the truth of this adversary system. My grandfather's case against John D. Rockefeller is an example of how the system can be sabotaged by shady lawyering. I describe in the first chapter how a crucial letter was withheld, which, if it had been produced under the discovery request, would surely have resulted in a settlement favorable to my grandfather during the trial or before. The unscrupulous switching of sides by attorney Joseph Cotton from the Merritt side to join the Rockefeller forces also played a role. If the 1947 hearings on the Silver Bay permits had been handled in a contested case hearing with lawyers on both sides armed with discovery demands, the testimony of Dr. Eddy withheld by William Montague, attorney for Reserve's predecessor, would have been presented by the Reserve opponents in an adversary context that would have altered the outcome of this massive tailings pollution of Lake Superior.

A number of years after I left the MPCA job, I was introduced to a private detective named Art Von Jr. at the Captain's Table in Duluth. As we drank coffee that morning, he told me an arresting but also amusing story. He said that during the height of the Reserve Company battle, Reserve's lawyer Ed Fride hired him to go to Isle Royale and check out our cabin and island in Tobin Harbor because Fride had been told that we were discharging sewage directly into Lake Superior. Von accepted the job and made the long trip in his boat to Tobin, where he quickly found that the pipe leading from our cabin to the water was our water intake pipe! Having dealt with Ed Fride over the years, I again concluded how aggressive he could be in advocating for his client. But I also got a laugh out of his effort in this incident.

A Lifetime of Change on Isle Royale

The love of water runs very deep in my life. Perhaps that is due to genes inherited from Grandfather Alfred Merritt, who spent years on Lake Superior before searching for iron ore on the Mesabi Range. He and his older brother Leonidas built the first commercial sailboat at the head of the lakes. They used this seventy-foot vessel, named the *Chaska,* and another that followed, the *Handy,* in trading on Lake Superior. For example, they hauled rock for the Ontonagan, Michigan, breakwater and lumber to Marquette, Michigan. Alfred Merritt was also the first tugboat captain at the Duluth harbor.

I made many trips with my family to Isle Royale from Grand Marais, Grand Portage, and Port Arthur (now Thunder Bay) in the 1940s and 1950s. In 1939 and 1941 we took the *Winyah* to our island in Tobin Harbor at the northeastern end of Isle Royale. Two memories of those two trips stand out even though I was only five and seven at the time. One was the way we drank water out of the lake while under way by swinging a cup out on a line from the lower deck. The other was when, in 1941, Captain Ole let me blow the whistle for the Rock Harbor Lodge as we were headed back to Grand Marais. After the *Winyah* was replaced in 1944 by the stubby former car ferry, the *Detroit,* we made our trips on the *Detroit* that year and the next, but when Dad learned that a converted Canadian sub chaser, the *Coastal Queen,* was to operate out of Port Arthur, Ontario, we rode the *Queen* in 1946, '47, and '48, until that beautiful 120-foot boat stopped its service. After that we took smaller boats, the *Disturbance,* and the *Voyageur,* out of Grand Portage. All of these trips meant many long hours of standing on deck watching water and fish go by and thinking about the immense body of water in Lake Superior. I'm sure that all this time on Lake Superior helped form my passion for taking action when the lake was threatened by pollution.

An early explorer with the initials of CAJ called this place "a great crown set around with islands for gems." Ingeborg Holte of Wright Island in Siskiwit Bay was the daughter of commercial fisherman Sam Johnson and the wife of commercial fisherman Ed Holte. Ingeborg said of Isle Royale, "I think the most exciting part of being on Isle Royale is going out on the water. It is a terrific feeling." I agree with her, and I suspect most boaters would as well.

Whether you approach Isle Royale from Copper Harbor, Michigan, Grand Portage, Minnesota, or Thunder Bay, Ontario, the island looms large and imposing. It extends fifty miles west from Gull Rocks beyond Passage Island to Rock of Ages, and it sinks into the horizon when you leave. At times it disappears into the fog like Brigadoon. The island is mystical—it is not like driving to or from another national park that is gone after the first turn in the road. There are no roads there. Sometimes from our island in Tobin Harbor a mirage magnifies the Gull Rocks. Where else can you see a national park as a mirage? Growing up on Isle Royale was like living in another world—a remote blue-green one with commercial fishermen and great sport fishing while drinking water right out of the lake, picking blueberries, going after birch trees downed by beaver who kindly left the end off the ground so the wood did not rot, and collecting pulp wood from beaches. A different life indeed. I remember what it was like as a seven-year-old learning how to steer the *Kalevala* with the stick on a chain running along the gunwale—do you go forward to back out left, or vice versa?

Growing up with time spent at a cabin surrounded on three sides with windows was very special. We still drink water right out of Lake Superior. We had no electricity and still use kerosene lamps. We cooked on a wood stove, and still use it. We now have a vintage Servel gas stove and refrigerator fueled by propane. And I grew up with an outhouse, which we still use. So we have tried to stay as close as possible to living like the pioneers of more than a hundred years ago.

We arrived on the *Winyah* in those pre–World War II years, after driving from our home in Duluth to catch the boat at Grand Marais, where we stayed in the old Arrowhead Hotel. On our way back home one trip, in 1941, as we neared the dock at Rock Harbor Lodge that year, I recall my dad, Glen Merritt, asking Captain Ole Berg how old "the Commodore" was, referring to Kneut Kneutson, the owner and founder of Park Place, which became Rock Harbor Lodge. Ole said, "Val, last year he vas ninety, this year he is ninety-five." That was one of my earliest introductions to cultural perspectives by the island folk.

One of my grandfather's first jobs was in 1866 as a nineteen-year-old deckhand on the schooner *Pierpont*. It stopped at Washington

Harbor, at the southwestern tip of Isle Royale, with 1,500 hundred-pound kegs for the commercial fishermen there, picking them up six weeks later filled with lake trout, whitefish, and herring, all salted down. He returned in 1873 in charge of a crew to build the two-and-one-half-mile road up the rugged terrain to the Island Mine from Siskiwit Bay, which they finished in 1874.

Then he went prospecting around the island for copper with Captain Samuel W. Hill, who could "swear a string of oaths a mile long." Hill is the reason for the expression "What the Sam Hill" according to local legend. After that Grandfather returned frequently with family members even during the two and a half years from 1887 to 1890 when he and other members of the family were busy searching with crews for iron ore on the Mesabi Iron Range, ending with the discovery at Mountain Iron on November 16, 1890.

In 1908 he attended the auction of islands at Marquette, Michigan. He bought a number of islands, including the four that are right inside and south of Blake's Point at the northeastern tip of Isle Royale. For three years early in the 1900s he cruised with his family to Isle Royale from Duluth in his forty-two-foot yacht, the *Jean M.*, named after his last child, who became Mrs. Milton Mattson of East Beaver Bay. The *Jean M.* had a tall mast and good-sized sail. It also had a ten-horsepower Campbell "make or break" engine. They stayed at Tourist Home, now Davidson Island in Rock Harbor.

On one trip around 1908 Grandfather went into Washington Harbor and docked at Barnum Island. As Grandfather and Dad were on the dock tying their ropes, they heard George Barnum Sr. come out of his cottage and yell at them: "Five dollars an hour to tie up at this dock!" Dad said Grandfather paid no attention and when Mr. Barnum got closer and recognized Grandfather he said, "Oh, is that you, Alf? You can tie up here anytime."

In 1911 Alfred and family built a large cabin in Tobin Harbor, on the first island south of Blake's Point that has access and views to the open lake to the east, with views of the sun and moon rises, and the calm waters of Merritt Lane to the west. This became Camp Comfort. Later he bought Wright's Island in Siskiwit Bay and a small island farther up Tobin Harbor from Al Ribenack, the owner of the Lenox Hotel in Duluth. When the park was created, the Alfred Merritt family had fourteen islands. The family sold all of them to the park for five dollars an acre, except the one up the harbor known as Camp Dig Inn, and obtained a life lease to occupy that island, which we still do under a special use permit. So my sister Mary Scheibe, together with her husband, Dick, her son, Brian Merritt Bergson, and my family have occupied this island almost every summer. Our three children and ten grandchildren have enjoyed being there virtually every summer as well.

The initial impetus for Isle Royale becoming a national park came in 1921 from a journalist at the *Detroit News*, Albert Stoll. The Stoll Trail from Rock Harbor Lodge to Scoville Point is named after him. One of his articles reached the Washington, D.C., desk of Stephen Mather, director of the National Park Service (NPS). Mather was impressed with the potential of Isle Royale as a national park, especially after he arranged a boat tour of the island in 1924.

When Isle Royale was established, landowners were given the choice of selling or taking life leases. Approximately twenty-five chose life leases and of that number only one life lease is left. Sixteen families have special use permits or volunteer-in-the-park permits. In 1982 I started a new organization, the Isle Royale Original Families Association, which is now the Isle Royale Families and Friends Association, known as IRFFA. We expanded the scope to include friends of Isle Royale at the suggestion of Jim Marshall, owner of the *Lake Superior* magazine. A chief objective of that organization is to somehow keep the present communities at the island together for the future in order to preserve the island's cultural history along with the historic structures for succeeding generations. Isle Royale National Park needs the presence of these original families as long as possible in order to keep the history of this magnificent place accurate and available to the visiting public.

For example, in the 2016 edition of the park's *Greenstone* magazine, a park ranger wrote a story claiming that an expedition of professional scientists visiting the island in 1928 was responsible for the NPS deciding that the island was suitable as a national park. The correct history is that the first NPS director, Stephen Mather, led a group of Isle Royale residents, landowners, conservationists, politicians, and businessmen four years earlier in 1924. That group included my grandfather, Alfred Merritt, from Tobin Harbor and George Barnum of Washington Harbor. Both of them favored making Isle Royale a national park. The group visited the entire island in a yacht owned by Thomas Cole, agent for the Island Copper Company. After this visit Mather determined that Isle Royale met all the criteria for a national park and supported the growing movement for its inclusion in the park system, which happened shortly after his death in 1930. The 2016 article by Val Martin should have been edited to correct this historical error, but nobody at the park caught the mistake. I noticed it right away and so did others of the original families.

Enabling legislation for the park was passed by Congress in 1931, and the park was officially dedicated in late August 1946 at park headquarters on Mott Island, with the cruise ship *South American* tied to the dock and a thousand spectators seated and standing on the dock or decks of the large ship. My sister, Mary Alice, our parents, and I were fortunate to be present for the dedication.

A number of unforgettable characters have been part of the fabric of the island. I will list those that I have known in my lifetime at our northeastern end. I have only heard about the many who came before me such as Dr. Maurice Edwards, preacher and great fly fisherman of Edwards Island who, along with all the Edwardses, are lineal descendants of Jonathan Edwards, the pre-Revolutionary theologian and the third president of Princeton University. He delivered the famous sermon "Sinners in the Hands of an Angry God." Here are those that I knew: my dad, Glen Merritt, Alfreda Gale, Elizabeth Kemmer, Art and Inez Mattson, Dr. Charles Parker Connolly, Henry Beard, Pete Edisen, Milford Johnson, and Westy Farmer.

There was one more—Roy J. Snell—and he lived right across the narrow channel from our island on the mainland, where his camp remains today. Roy Snell was the author of eighty-six children's books and many magazine articles, and wrote *The Jack Armstrong* radio show for a time. He lectured with 16 mm movies about Isle Royale around Chicago, where he lived, and the Detroit area.

He grew up in Wheaton, Illinois, and went to Wheaton College, an evangelical college that Billy Graham attended. But when he left for a job in Alaska he didn't last long with religion.

The reason I call him an unforgettable character was the way he fished. He had one of the old sixteen-foot Thompson rowboats. He always rowed with alternating rowing strokes. He would row out and fish all day from the time he left his dock until he returned. All by himself. By the time I was a teenager he would take me along. One day we went out in his boat. By this time he had a small outboard. We headed right out to Five Foot Reef and promptly hit a huge school of fish. In a half hour we caught fifty-five pounds of lake trout. I caught the biggest one—seventeen pounds. That's still the biggest I've ever caught. And we had no net, just a gaff hook. After that we went to Blake's Point but had no luck there. So we decided to have lunch on one of the beaches toward Locke Point. At that time Mr. Snell was about seventy and I was sixteen. After lunch he began singing songs such as "Moonlight and Roses." And then he said "Now, Grant, it's time to meditate on the realities of the absolute." And he wasn't talking about Absolut vodka.

Our Tobin Harbor friend and fisherman Art Mattson wrote a short poem for Marilyn and me in 1962 upon my graduation from law school. It came with a beautiful model sailboat that he carved out of one of his cedar net buoys and named *Lovers Lane,* which is a lane in Tobin Harbor. Here is that poem:

We all have dreams of sailing away,
To some distant lands at the break of day.
So, hoist up the sails, and bring her around,
For "Lovers Lane" is outward bound.

That little poem captures the feeling many of us have as we head for "the Island."

Isle Royale has become renowned in the past thirty-plus years for wolves and moose. But there is so much more to this island archipelago. There is a rich cultural history, including commercial fishermen, mining and logging, resorts, summer residents, among them some remaining unforgettable people, boating and navigation, the hiking trails and camping facilities as well as the history of how a national park was created and developed on this 134,000 acres and over four hundred surrounding islands. Those of us who have spent virtually every summer at the island, either as life lessees or boaters, have had a love and sometimes less than a love relationship with the NPS, which sometimes has not treated the life residents very kindly. Art Sivertson, Howard Sivertson's fisherman father, had a medical problem that necessitated spending the summer in Duluth. When he got back to Washington Harbor the next year he found that his special use permit had been canceled by the Park Service never to be recovered, with the park saying he forfeited it because he did not fish that one season. The Isle Royale commercial fishermen should have had life leases, but because they were squatters they had no warranty deeds to show when the park was created. Only three out of all the Isle Royale fishermen had title and therefore life leases—Art Mattson of Tobin Harbor, Emil Anderson of Belle Isle, and Sam Sivertson, Art and Stanley Sivertson's father. Most of the rest, however, had been there at least fifteen years and, therefore, had adverse possession.

The Michigan acquisition agent told several families in the 1930s that they could not include their minor children on the life leases, which was not true. Since I was one of those children, and a lawyer as well as active in politics, I challenged the park on this and after some twenty years of fighting for the right to be on the life lease, I finally prevailed. This benefited not only my sister and me, but six other families with minor children when their life leases were signed. The solution came about when my mother said, "You know the politicians, why not get them to help?" So we did. I asked then Senator Mondale to introduce a bill to revise and reform our family life lease in order to add my sister and me. Staffer Mike Berman worked on the bill and Senator Mondale and I testified in two separate sessions of Senate committees to urge passage. Fritz Mondale was successful in passing the bill in both the 1971 and 1973 sessions.

Congressman Don Fraser introduced the same bill in the House of Representatives, but when it was not moving along, the new superintendent of Isle Royale, Jack Morehead, in 1977 proposed a compromise, which we accepted, that granted us and the other families special use permits for twenty years, renewable if we are still living. The only differences with the life leases we sought were a charge of twenty-five dollars a year and a prohibition on visiting our island in the winter. I very much appreciated what Fritz Mondale did for us in paving the way for the minor children who should have been on their families' life leases to continue at Isle Royale.

In the late 1990s, many of the regular boaters coming to the island every summer became upset with the proposed General Management Plan of the park, particularly the parts calling for removal of docks, extensive and sometimes unnecessary no-wake zones, and removal of the trail along the south side of Lake Richie that enables boaters and hikers to access the Greenstone Ridge Trail from Chippewa Harbor.

The Isle Royale Boaters Association challenged that plan in federal district court knowing that a lawsuit against the National Park Service rarely prevails. I acted as their lawyer at the trial court level and the case went all the way to the Sixth Circuit Court of Appeals, only to end with another victory for the park. However, the NPS has yet to take out the Siskiwit dock or the Three Mile dock in Rock Harbor and has decided not to remove the south Lake Richie trail. So the lawsuit did end up accomplishing three of the five major objectives we sought.

Isle Royale has always evolved with changes just as the rest of the earth. I have seen over the past sixty years changes especially in the vegetation, the water levels, and the fishery. The big change in the past several years is in the climate. The year 2010 was very hot followed by the same thing in 2011 and 2012. The water temperature off our dock, which is two miles west of Blake's Point, has averaged 70–71 degrees for those years during late July and August.

Because of the invasion of both lamprey and smelt, the lake trout changed dramatically over the past sixty years. In the 1940s lake trout fed mostly on herring and were a fine lean fish. With the lamprey predation in the late 1940s and 1950s, lake trout were nearly eradicated at Isle Royale. Once Dow Chemical developed a means to poison lamprey larvae, the Isle Royale lake trout bounced back by the late 1960s. And then the smelt took over as the main diet of lake trout, which caused them to increase in belly size from the lean trout we previously caught. During that time, I can recall cleaning a five- or six-pound laker with seven smelt in its stomach. Most of the trout over five pounds were too fat to eat. No longer did we see schools of herring around the island. In those days, the herring were attacked by both the lamprey and the smelt.

By the early 1990s the herring returned, but it wasn't long before thousands of cormorants descended and soon the herring population took another nosedive. One spring I saw seagulls and cormorants in large numbers in Tobin Harbor. They seemed to get along well. And then I realized that the aggressive seagulls were grabbing the cormorants by the neck, causing them to lose their catch to the seagulls. After the cormorants caused the big dip in the herring population, they left the island with only a few stragglers remaining. Now the herring are in schools again around the island.

The island vegetation has changed dramatically as well. The moose and the beaver have reduced the population of birch and aspen, which have been replaced by spruce and balsam. Moose have also shown a keen interest in eating small white pine but leave red pine alone. In 1953 Lou Mattson and I transplanted over a dozen white pine and one red pine from Duncan Bay Creek on our island and at his place. The moose ate most of the white pine and the rest died from other causes. The one red pine has survived, however, and grown from a seedling of about three inches to a beautiful and healthy pine of about sixty-five feet tall. I planted it next to our trail on the south side of the island and have felt it was my sole "tree farm." In 2012 I discovered several offspring growing from that huge tree. As of 2017 I counted three young red pines along the south shore, two of which are up to four feet tall.

Scientists are predicting that the warmer weather will result in savanna forest trees such as basswood, birch, maple, and aspen replacing the boreal forest. With the warmer weather and longer summer and fall, the moose are being plagued with ticks, causing them to rub off their fur before going into the winter season. As a result they are weakened and easier prey for the wolves. The wolf numbers were down to two by 2016.

Isle Royale moose arrived on the island around 1910. They either came over themselves or were brought there by humans. The old-timers, like my father, said they walked over during the winter of 1910–11. Recently, wildlife managers and biologists have disputed this, claiming moose do not walk far on ice because their sharp hooves cause them to skid and fall on ice.[6] Moose could walk on the ice bridges, however, if they were covered with snow, which often occurs. Another explanation is that the moose were taken over on barges from Two Harbors. One evening sitting at our campfire in Tobin Harbor with Dr. and Mrs. Lyman Clay of Minneapolis, Dr. Clay told us the following story. In 1930 he and his wife were driving through Manitoba when they had to stay overnight while their car was repaired. The next morning as they were leaving, the owner of the service station asked where they were going. When he heard it was Isle Royale, he said he took a herd of moose over to Washington Harbor in a barge from Two Harbors! So the speculation on how they got there goes on. Regardless of how the moose arrived, they took hold and thrived.

Wolves came over from the North Shore in 1948 and for decades there was a renowned "balance of nature" between the wolves and moose on the island until around 2010. Caribou had occupied Isle Royale since well before the moose and coexisted with them until 1934, when the famous wildlife artist Les Kouba observed the last caribou.[7] Due to drought and climate change, and perhaps other factors, the lake level has been low in recent years. Large clumps of grass are now observed growing along many shorelines.

By 2015 the levels had returned to normal, but the grass is still growing. Obviously, change will continue in some ways even if we reduce the carbon dioxide being emitted around the world. But reducing these emissions can minimize the direct results of the warmer climate. Water levels and temperatures should normalize and once again lake trout will be swimming closer to the surface in cooler waters. We should be moving much faster to deal with climate change. And if we do, Isle Royale will be the better for the change.

I still treasure the deep-blue water and sky and the summer squalls. But those squalls can be treacherous. One day in August 1960, Marilyn and I, with friends Dave and Lavon Priebe, were boating on the north side beyond Locke Point. We picnicked on a calm afternoon after fishing and looking for zeolite stones. As we motored in the lee of the mainland toward Blake Point, I noticed the trees at the point were bent way over with a raging south-easter under way. After weighing the options, I decided our sturdy eighteen-foot wooden boat, the *Handy*, could make it around the short distance to Merritt Lane. After all, I knew it was sturdy since I had watched it being built on Park Point in Duluth in 1947. So we pulled up the canvas spray hood, had our friends sit in the bow under the hood, and Marilyn held on to my belt as we came around the point. Eight-foot waves broke over the spray hood. Marilyn held on to me for dear life and we made it to the safety of those calm Merritt Lane waters.

I have had the pleasure of experiencing travel to the island in many different boats and even sailing around some of the island in sailboats and antique crafts such as the *HMS*, owned by the Tobin's Harbor Gale family, and formerly by Henry M. Scofield, owner of the Belle Isle Resort. As I said earlier, for three years in the 1940s, when I was a youngster, my family took the *Coastal Queen* out of Port Arthur. On the first trip in 1946 we headed for Belle Isle, where we lunched in the lodge during its last year of operation. The entire trip to Rock Harbor only took two and a half hours travel on the converted submarine chaser.

It was quite a letdown to have to go back to taking the *Detroit*, referred to as the "Pickle Boat," out of Grand Marais, where we often left at 5:00 a.m. and did not arrive in Tobin's Harbor until 7:00 p.m. On one trip we left at 3:45 a.m. and since the *Detroit* only went

8.5 mph, it took thirty-five minutes from Grand Marais Harbor to 5 Mile Rock. I think the Brigadoon feeling struck me as we slowly rode along to and from Grand Marais because the island would gradually rise and fall as we proceeded ever so slowly.

In mid-September 1951, Dad and I returned to Grand Marais on the *Detroit*. We had to lay over in Washington Harbor for a day after riding a sea so high in a thirty-five-mile-an-hour wind that I figured we were at a forty-five-degree angle riding up the waves and then the stubby boat would pound so hard the dishes would fly off the shelves in the galley. We left Washington Harbor for the fifty-four-mile trip to Grand Marais at night in calmer waters heading into the sparkling path of a full moon moving faster to the west than we were.

On another occasion, when we were teenagers, my boyhood pal at the island, Art and Inez Mattson's son Louis and I were invited to accompany Carl and Lucy Dassler on their twenty-six-foot wooden cruiser *Awanita* from Tobin to Copper Harbor. The Dasslers had the camp with the same name as the Ely, Minnesota, camp of the famous Sigurd Olson—Listening Point, just north of Scoville Point, which is now the location of the Artist-in-Residence program. Lou and I spent two days exploring the tip of the Keweenaw Peninsula, and then on the way back in the fog we had some real excitement. As we approached the steamship lanes in this 1948 trip we had only a fog whistle, which we blew every minute, a compass and a radio direction finder to guide us. You couldn't see a hundred feet, and at that point I was steering. Suddenly, an ore boat loomed right ahead. Captain Dassler ordered hard to the port. As I whipped the wheel to the west to go past the stern, the freighter's captain started blowing his whistle. It was then we noticed they were pulling a "log line" behind the stern to record their speed, and while crew members ran to the stern waving at us we steered farther out and passed by without cutting their log line.

In 1963, on a nice August day, Marilyn and I were heading back to Grand Portage on the *Voyageur* with Roy Oberg at the helm and Merle Otto as engineer. Along the north side of the island west of Little Todd Harbor, the engine started giving trouble. Roy spotted it—a rumbling in the drive shaft. He immediately shut down the engine and we were floating along about a mile from shore. Luckily there was little wind and it was from the west. There were twenty-three passengers on board that small boat. Suddenly Roy walked to the bow and hoisted a piece of tarp on a pole and announced, "We're going to do a little sailing here, just like my grandfather did. Line up two trees on shore and you'll see we're going about a mile an hour! Meanwhile I'll try to get hold of the Park Service."

Not much luck; it was a Sunday afternoon and nobody was home. During this time the Grand Marais Coast Guard radioed Captain Oberg: "Your wife is in the hospital in Grand Marais and is going to have a baby—get here immediately!"

The Park Service finally heard the calls and arrived with a small boat that towed us to Washington Harbor. That took several hours and from there all of us were transferred to another Sivertson boat, the *Hiawatha*. By the time we arrived in Grand Portage it was 6:00 p.m. As quickly as we could we packed the car and drove Roy to the hospital. He did not seem to be worried along the way, telling us stories with his trademark laugh. We got to the hospital and discovered it was false labor!

In May 1991, a group of five made a trip to Isle Royale, as we had done since 1988, and enjoyed fine lake trout fishing at the head of Tobin Harbor. While we were fishing from the twenty-six-foot Bertram *Jamada* with owner Jim Pedersen, his son David mentioned there was a large tract of wilderness land and a small lake called Lost Lake for sale by the Trust for Pubic Land. It was just over a thousand acres. Consolidated Paper Company owned the land and had sold it to the TPL. Consolidated had harvested white pine there but had saved most of the pine around the lake as well as seed trees away from the lake. I was intrigued, so when we returned to Grand Portage from Isle Royale I sought out my cousin John Henry Eliasen Jr. in Grand Marais, who knew the property and location. He gave me a good map. I drove up the same morning we had returned from Isle Royale. It was difficult to get to the lake. When I arrived I was exhausted after our trip back from the island that morning, so I had a quick lunch and took a nap in the woods above the west end of the lake. When I awoke, I looked around and saw hundreds of white pine seedlings and a beautiful little lake looking very much like the Boundary Waters. It was hard not to fall in love with the place. The area looked so appealing that I thought it was worth buying—if I could. After spending time walking around some of the property, I drove back to Grand Marais and looked up John Dietrick, whose real estate company had the listing for the TPL.

After negotiations, and several trips back there from the Twin Cities, I was able to buy the entire tract for a good price, with a down payment from my 401(k) retirement fund and note and mortgage. Backwoods land like this was not selling well at the time, and for six or seven years thereafter, but I was able to make the mortgage payments, pay the property taxes, and take steps to sell some lots on the lake and out-lots away from the lake with an easement to use the lake. My purpose was to try to replicate our Isle Royale experience as closely as possible and pass on the wilderness to others and our family, something I cannot do at Isle Royale unless the National Park Service decides to allow the few remaining families to stay.

The purchase agreement with TPL provided that no more than twelve lots could be sold on Lost Lake and that they must conform to the 150-foot setback of the DNR as a natural environment lake. The zoning that Consolidated Paper had for the lake was FAR-1 (forest, agriculture and recreation), which called for 600 feet of shoreline and twenty acres of land for each parcel. These were larger lots than normal for lakes in Cook County. With the professional help of our realtor, Mike Raymond, president of Red Pine Realty, we sold eight lake lots, saved one for ourselves, and created a conservation easement on most of the south side of the lake which allows only a trail on those forty-four acres.

During the twenty-plus years of ownership since, my family and I have spent many pleasant times at this wilderness land and lake, fishing and hunting, swimming and hiking. We have enjoyed the beauty of the spring marsh marigolds and the moose and bear who occasionally cross our path. Our fellow Lost Lake Retreat owners have become friends who also enjoy the nature and wilderness values of this special place. We are creating a new mixture of a few like-minded folks in this wilderness area, which is just north of Judge C. R. Magney State Park. I think of the Trust for Public Land motto we learned when we bought this gem of land and lake: "Habitat isn't just for wildlife." My goals for Isle Royale and Lost Lake reflect that belief. TPL also says, "Humans need healthy open spaces, too." Young children already coming into contact with the natural world at Lost Lake will retain values learned there the rest of their lives. We will do our part to save our children from what author Richard Louv calls "nature-deficit disorder."[8] Human interactions with nature are vital to our planet's future.

EPILOGUE

In 1981 my family and I headed for Hawaii for a conference of motor carrier lawyers on the Big Island. We combined that with visits first to Oahu to see fellow Isle Royale life lessees Don and Florence Wolbrink in Honolulu and then to spend several days on Maui and from there to the Kona Surf area of the big island of Hawaii for the conference. After the meetings were over we rented a car and drove to the north and then between Mauna Kea and Mauna Loa, where we stopped to see Volcano National Park. On the way back to the hotel we stopped at Kealakekua Bay near the "Little Grass Shack" made famous by entertainer Arthur Godfrey. I wanted to see this site because I had dinner with Mr. Godfrey in Duluth when he visited Reserve Mining in 1974. It was a memorable dinner at the revolving top of the Duluth Radisson Hotel attended by Chuck Stoddard and Godfrey's journalist friends Mr. and Mrs. Robert Cahn.

We arrived on a Saturday at the dock in the bay, which was extraordinary because it had no condos or development whatsoever. We were fortunate in summoning the owner of the glass-bottom boat moored at the dock. He appeared to be a native Hawaiian and consented to take us over to the Captain Cook Monument. On the way back he went down below and came up with a mess of squid and other fish food, then dove off the boat and fed the fish—which appeared from all over at the sight of him.

After he was done and back on the deck, I asked him how far down you could see in these waters. He said about 140 feet. I was quite surprised and said, "Back home in Lake Superior waters we think being able to see forty feet down is quite an accomplishment." Without a moment's delay he said, "Oh, I thought they paved that lake over with taconite tailings!" I almost fell off the boat.

"How did you hear about those taconite tailings being dumped in Lake Superior?" I asked.

He said, "I studied that case while taking a master's degree in marine biology from Captain Jacques Cousteau."

I briefly related my years of fighting the dumping of those tailings and asked him what he was doing running a glass-bottom boat here in Kealakekua Bay. He said he came back here to his home to see if he could prevent the bay from being "condoized" like so many other bays on his native island. Since I had spent thirteen years on the Reserve case and then more on the later discharge from Milepost 7 into Lake Superior via Beaver River, I could understand how this native Hawaiian was working to save his home.

What a coincidence: he left a career in marine biology to return home to help save the environment, and he thought so much of the water and land that inspired him to study ecology that he came back to fight for its future. He had a teacher who gave him an example of how such a fight was worth giving up a lucrative pursuit, at least for a time, to begin a battle against those who were going to threaten his core values and homeland. I leave my story with the conviction that a fight to save your homeland that you love so much is well worth the effort.

The battle goes on—on Lake Superior, in Hawaii, and around the world.

ACKNOWLEDGMENTS

When I started this project I was planning to do two things: correct the history of my family's involvement with John D. Rockefeller and write my recollections of the monumental Reserve Mining Company case that consumed so much of my life for nearly twenty years. I soon recognized that I had more history to record about protecting the environment, so this book is now a history of my family in mining as well as an account of citizen advocacy and fighting for the environment. It is a memoir of my life spent pursuing these goals.

I have had help in these efforts going back to my grade school teachers at Washburn in Duluth, which include Misses Clark and Foster. My parents, Alice and Glen Merritt, encouraged me to understand history and politics at a very early age. They helped me prepare a pennant full of Franklin Roosevelt buttons from his presidential campaigns of 1932, '36, '40, and '44 and pin it on the front door during the election of 1944, when I was ten years old, and they urged me to read the book about my family, *Seven Iron Men*, by Paul de Kruif, when I was in the eighth grade. They had me take dramatic-reading lessons during seventh grade and encouraged me to become an entrepreneur with a paper route carrying the morning *Duluth News–Tribune* for three and a half years.

At Duluth Central High School I benefited from working with Miss Maybelle Hoyt, who was our student council adviser when I was council president, and George Beck, principal at Central, who was an inspiration during my three years there. In my four years of undergraduate study at the University of Minnesota Duluth, I was fortunate to be a student of the political science faculty of Gerhard von Glahn, Julius Fred Wolff, and Emmett Davidson. At the

Acknowledgments

Public Administration Center I had more great teachers, the most memorable being Walter Heller, who later served as chairman of the Council of Economic Advisers under Presidents John Kennedy and Lyndon Johnson. At the University of Minnesota Law School, Dean Lockhart, Yale Kamisar, Al McCoid, Jim Hetland, and Jim Hogg were professors of importance in molding my career.

At the beginning of this book project and through all these years of writing, I was very fortunate that a noted author, David Dempsey, advised and encouraged me. He helped me in my writing, stressing conciseness (i.e., shorter sentences). As I began working with the University of Minnesota Press, my first editor was Todd Orjala, followed by Erik Anderson. They have been great editors and wonderful to work with. One summer I rewrote portions of the manuscript following instructions from Erik and the other editors at the University of Minnesota Press on a fifty-year-old Royal manual typewriter at Isle Royale—we have no electricity or Wi-Fi out there in the middle of Lake Superior. At the suggestion of the Press I hired a professional developmental editor, Gordon Thomas, who encouraged me to expand my treatment of Judge Miles Lord, Governor Wendell Anderson, and others. He was very helpful and well worth the investment.

Along the way my wife, Marilyn, made good suggestions and was most patient with the time it took to complete the manuscript.

NOTES

Much of the material in this book is drawn from my experiences over fifty years of public service. More information can be found in the Grant J. Merritt Papers (1947–1984) located at the Minnesota Historical Society in St. Paul, Minnesota.

Prologue

1. Grant J. Merritt Papers, 1947–1984, box 2, file 4, Minnesota Historical Society.

The Merritt Family and the Mesabi Iron Range

1. Alfred Merritt, "Reminiscences," 7. Personal memoir from our family's collection.

2. Ibid., 9.

3. Paul de Kruif, *Seven Iron Men: The Merritts and the Discovery of the Mesabi Range* (1929; repr., Minneapolis: University of Minnesota Press, 2007), 157.

4. *Twentieth Annual Report of the Minnesota Geological and Natural History Survey,* 113.

5. David A. Walker, *Iron Frontier: The Discovery and Early Development of Minnesota's Three Ranges* (1979; repr., St. Paul: Minnesota Historical Society Press, 2004), 100–101.

6. Ibid., 100–105; de Kruif, *Seven Iron Men,* 185.

7. Frank A. King, *The Missabe Road: The Duluth, Missabe and Iron Range Railway* (1972; repr., Minneapolis: University of Minnesota Press, 2003), 48.

8. Walker, *Iron Frontier*, 105–6.

9. King, *Missabe Road*, 111.

10. Ibid., 75.

11. Joseph Wilmer Thompson, "An Economic History of the Mesabi Division of the Great Northern Railway Company to 1915" (Ph.D. dissertation, University of Illinois at Urbana–Champaign, 1956).

12. Walker, *Iron Frontier*, 117.

13. Ibid., 186.

14. Ron Chernow, *Titan: The Life of John D. Rockefeller, Sr.* (New York: Random House, 1998), 385 and n. 86.

15. Allan Nevins, *Study in Power: John D. Rockefeller, Industrialist and Philanthropist.* 2 vols. (New York: Charles Scribner's Sons, 1953).

16. Mr. Nevins and my father, Glen Merritt, as well as two of his sisters, engaged in considerable correspondence with him. I have copies of all those letters. Mr. Nevins's responses indicate that he wrote this story believing that Gates told the truth. He said he had "great confidence in the integrity and accuracy of Mr. Gates." My dad said in a reply to Nevins that Rockefeller "even made a desperate attempt to withdraw these ore properties (Rockefeller's) from the (joint consolidation) in January of 1894 and this can be proven by a glance at the records of this trial, which are all available here in the files of the District Court."

17. Merritt, *Reminiscences*, 10.

18. Letter from Glen J. Merritt to Allan Nevins, author's private archive.

19. *Duluth Herald,* June 29, 1951, 1.

20. *St. Paul Pioneer Press,* November 17, 1990.

21. Thompson, "An Economic History," 204–13. A letter dated February 7, 1899, in the James J. Hill collection from D. M. Philbin to James N. Hill and forwarded to James J. Hill, shows that Philbin was working for the Hill interests; personal visits by the author with his father Glen J. Merritt and Albro Martin, author of the biography of James J. Hill.

22. *New York World* magazine, February 18, 1917, 1.

23. *New York World* magazine, February 25, 1917, 1.

24. Don W. Larson, *Land of the Giants: A History of Minnesota Business* (Minneapolis: Dorn Books, 1979), 100.

25. Andrus Merritt, *The Story of the Mesabi* (1934), 259–62. Manuscript collection, Minnesota Historical Society, St. Paul.

26. Chernow, *Titan,* 392–93.

27. Theodore C. Blegen, *Minnesota: A History of the State.* 2nd ed. (Minneapolis: University of Minnesota Press, 1975), 366.

28. Norman K. Risjord, *A Popular History of Minnesota* (St. Paul: Minnesota Historical Society Press, 2005), 139.

29. Ibid.

30. Marvin G. Lamppa, *Minnesota's Iron Country: Rich Ore, Rich Lives* (Duluth: Lake Superior Port Cities, 2004), 120.

31. Interview with Glen J. Merritt, circa 1970.

32. Robert V. Bartlett, *The Reserve Mining Controversy: Science, Technology, and Environmental Quality* (Bloomington: Indiana University Press, 1980), 56.

Environmentalism and the Reserve Mining Controversy

1. Milton and Kermit's father, Edward Mattson, was a commercial fisherman who built the two-story log home adjacent to the dock, which is now on the National Register of Historic Buildings.

2. Author's journal, November 5, 1967.

3. Ibid.

4. The plank became part of the printed DFL party platform for 1968.

5. Thomas F. Bastow, *This Vast Pollution: United States of America v. Reserve Mining Company* (Washington, D.C.: Green Fields Books, 1986), 6–7.

6. Ibid., 8.

7. Stanley Ulrich, Timothy J. Berg, and Deborah Hedlund, *Superior Polluter* (Duluth: Save Lake Superior and Northern Environmental Council, 1972), 10.

8. Permits issued on December 18 and 22, 1947, by the Minnesota Department of Conservation and the Water Pollution Control Commission to Reserve Mining Company.

9. Bartlett, *The Reserve Mining Controversy,* 60–61.

10. Bastow, *This Vast Pollution,* 21.

11. Personal conference with David Durenberger, May 7, 2014.

12. Bastow, *This Vast Pollution,* 36.

13. Ulrich, Berg, and Hedlund, *Superior Polluter,* 9.

14. Ibid., 10

15. Ibid., 11.

16. Bartlett, *The Reserve Mining Controversy,* 82.

17. Bastow, *This Vast Pollution,* 43–44.

18. Ibid., 44.

19. River Falls, Wisconsin, newspaper.

20. Bartlett, *The Reserve Mining Controversy*, 103.

21. Interview with Tom Kelm's daughter, Michelle Kelm-Helgen, deputy chief of staff to Governor Mark Dayton, on February 7, 2012; John Earl Haynes, *Dubious Alliance: The Making of Minnesota's DFL Party* (Minneapolis: University of Minnesota Press, 1984), chapter 7, "The Road to Merger," 109–11.

22. Interview with former commissioner Richard Brubaker, March 12, 2012.

23. Memo from Kelm to me in box 2, file "Reserve Mining 5." Grant J. Merritt Papers, 1947–84, Minnesota Historical Society.

24. Interview with Brubaker, March 12, 2012.

25. Governor Wendell R. Anderson, Special Message to the Legislature of Minnesota, April 1, 1971, *Restoring and Preserving Minnesota's Environment*.

26. *Superior Polluter*, 152; April 22, 1971, conference, fol. 2, 126–27.

27. David Zwick and Marcy Benstock, *Water Wasteland* (New York: Grossman Publishers, 1971), 140–66.

28. Personal conversation with Byron Starns, Minneapolis, circa 2011.

29. When I interviewed Senator Rosenmeier's former aide, Blair Klein, I learned that the senator did not author a lot of bills in his long career in the Senate, but rather worked on institutional reforms. One of his strongest legacies is the creation of the Office of Senate Counsel in 1967. Senator Rosenmeier appointed Blair Klein the first senate counsel and chief of this new senate office, which Rosenmeier insisted must be independent of the political parties. Klein hired the first assistant senate counsel lawyers, among whom were Peter Wattson, David Kennedy, and Bruce Campbell. Wattson followed Klein and remained as chief counsel for many years. The senate counsel duties are to provide legal and technical services to the Senate and staff its committees.

30. Hearings before the Committee on Public Works, House of Representatives, Ninety-Second Congress, Dec. 9, 1971, 495–97.

31. "The Energy to Make Things Better, an Illustrated History of Northern States Power Company" (2000), 183, where I said, "Bob Engels was probably my favorite NSP president . . . because he pledged that NSP would meet the state standards at Prairie Island, even if he didn't have to do it legally."

32. Bastow, *This Vast Pollution*; Bartlett, *The Reserve Mining Controversy*.

33. Train v. City New York, 420 U.S. 35, 43 L.E. Led. 2d 1; Train v. Campaign Clean Water, Inc., 420 U.S. 136, 43 L. E. 2d 82 (1975).

34. Personal communication with Ron Paolin, of the Ontario Ministry of the Environment in Sudbury, May 31, 2017. Paolin reported that the SO2 is just 5 percent of the daily level of 4,400 tons when I was there in 1974.

35. Bastow, *This Vast Pollution*, 148.

36. Ibid., 150–51.

37. Ibid., 166.

38. Charles Hatch Stoddard, *Looking Forward: Planning America's Future* (New York: Macmillan, 1982), xvii.

Citizen Activist

1. Susan Jezsik Varlamoff, *The Polluters: A Community Strikes Back* (Edina, Minn.: St. John's Publishing, 1998).

2. 86 N.W. 882 (Minn. 1901).

3. Order, p. 13.

4. The testimony in a Fride document dated March 12 and 16, box 2, folder 4, Grant J. Merritt Papers, 1947–1984, Minnesota Historical Society; also the twenty-one statements from fishermen and residents along the shore. Box 2, folder 2, 1969–1970, Grant J. Merritt Papers, 1947–1984, Minnesota Historical Society.

5. D. Perry Kidder, "Did Taconite Save the Iron Range?," *Roots*, Spring 1989, 23.

6. Chel Anderson and Adelheid Fischer, *North Shore: A Natural History of Minnesota's Superior Coast* (Minneapolis: University of Minnesota Press, 2015), 510–11.

7. Personal communication with the artist.

8. Richard Louv, *Last Child in the Woods: Saving Our Children from Nature-Deficit Disorder* (Chapel Hill, N.C.: Algonquin Books, 2005).

INDEX

Page numbers in italics indicate photographs. All locations are in Minnesota unless otherwise specified.

Grant J. Merritt is a noted conservationist and attorney in the areas of environmental law, transportation, and land use. He has worked to protect the waters and wilderness of Minnesota for more than fifty years. In 1971 he was appointed by Governor Wendell Anderson as the executive director of the Minnesota Pollution Control Agency, a position he held until 1975. He served on the board of the Minnesota Environmental Quality Council and was Minnesota's representative on the Great Lakes Water Quality Board.